THE
CRUSADES

THE TWO HUNDRED YEARS WAR:
The Clash Between the Cross and the
Crescent in the Middle East 1096–1291

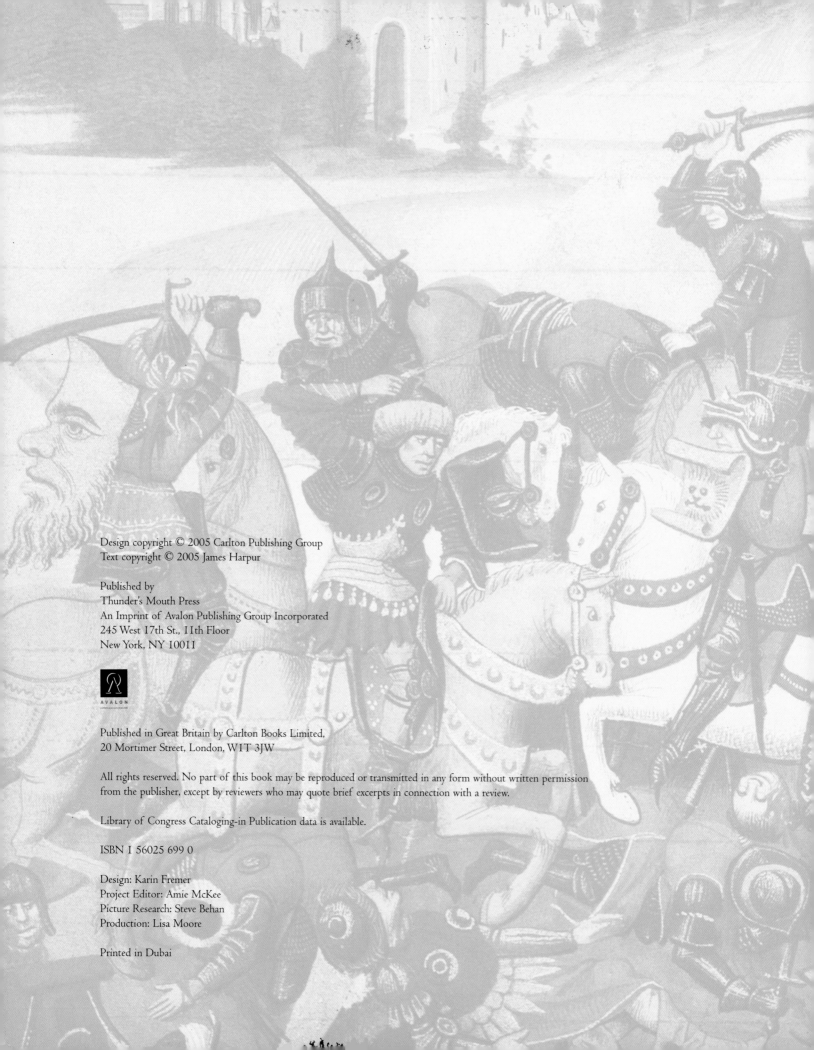

Design copyright © 2005 Carlton Publishing Group
Text copyright © 2005 James Harpur

Published by
Thunder's Mouth Press
An Imprint of Avalon Publishing Group Incorporated
245 West 17th St., 11th Floor
New York, NY 10011

Published in Great Britain by Carlton Books Limited,
20 Mortimer Street, London, W1T 3JW

Library of Congress Cataloging-in Publication data is available.

ISBN 1 56025 699 0

Design: Karin Fremer
Project Editor: Amie McKee
Picture Research: Steve Behan
Production: Lisa Moore

Printed in Dubai

THE
CRUSADES
AN ILLUSTRATED HISTORY

JAMES HARPUR

THUNDER'S
MOUTH
PRESS

CONTENTS

ABOVE *With the blessing of a group monks, the French king Louis IX sets out on crusade with his knights and retainers in this late medieval illumination.*

THE CRUSADES

In 1394 an Italian traveller named Martoni was visiting Cyprus when he was surprised to see that the well-to-do women of the island were wearing black clothes from head to toe, with only their eyes showing. When he inquired about the origin of this dress code he was informed that the women were symbolically mourning the capture by the Muslims of the Christian city of Acre on the Palestinian coast. What was extraordinary was that Acre had been lost more than a century ago, in 1291. But its fall to a Mamluk army from Egypt had a tremendous significance, because it marked the end of a 200-year Christian presence in Syria and Palestine (which historians usually label the "Latin east" or "Outremer", from the French for "beyond the sea").

OPPOSITE *Christ leads an army of crusaders into battle in this 14th-century French illustration from the Book of Revelation.*

From 1099 to 1291, crusaders from western Europe had established themselves in a region that had been under Muslim control since the rise and expansion of Islam in the seventh century AD. The crusaders, or *Franj* ("Franks") as they were called by the Muslims, were drawn to their epic expeditions of conquest by a mixture of motives (see Chapter Two), not least by a burning desire to liberate Jerusalem and the Holy Land from the infidel. As well as holding out the attractive prospect of power, money and land, the crusades were at heart profoundly religious and idealistic enterprises, having the character of a pilgrimage. They were sanctioned by popes, and those hardy souls who "took the cross" had to swear a solemn vow to make their journey. If they then defaulted, they were liable to excommunication – being cast out from the church, with all the spiritual perils that entailed. Crusaders, like pilgrims, were also granted papal indulgences, which assured them of a remission of penance due to sin – an enormous reward in an age when people were anxious about the afterlife, with its all-too-real categories of hell, purgatory and heaven.

The crusades to the east began after Pope Urban II, in 1095, called for a great expedition to help the Christian Byzantine Greeks, under pressure from the Seljuk Turks, and to liberate Jerusalem and the Holy Land from the Muslims. The First Crusade eventually got under way a year later and ended triumphantly with the Christians' capture of Jerusalem in 1099. The crusaders established four main states, namely the counties of Edessa and Tripoli, the principality of Antioch, and the kingdom of Jerusalem. The problem then was how to maintain these states in the face of Muslim hostility and a shortage of manpower, never satisfactorily resolved by the constant arrival of further adventurers and settlers from the west. That the Franks managed to remain in the east for nearly 200 years is a testament to their determination, tenacity and martial prowess, as well as to the way the spiritual allure of the Holy Land was constantly able to attract material assistance from Europe.

After the First Crusade there were other major expeditions (which, by convention, are numbered) as well as countless smaller ones. The Second Crusade was launched in 1147 to retake Edessa after it had fallen to the Muslims three years earlier. The Third Crusade was prompted by the loss of Jerusalem to the great Muslim general Saladin in 1187, while the Fourth Crusade (1202–04) ended up with the capture and pillaging of the Byzantine capital of Constantinople. The crusades in the thirteenth century included two expeditions to Egypt, perceived as the weak spot in the Muslims' defences, as well as an abortive attempt by Louis IX, king of France, to take Tunis. In the end, despite the threat of the Mongols, whose empire was steadily expanding westward from its central Asian heartland, the Muslim Mamluk dynasty in Egypt succeeded in driving the Christians from Outremer for good.

The crusades continue to hold a fascination for the west. This is partly due to a long process of romanticization and mythologizing (for example through the writings of Sir Walter Scott, such as *Ivanhoe*) that has crystallized and made popular images of knights in shining armour, chivalric behaviour and feats of derring-do. But for the reader who comes to accounts of the crusades with rose-tinted spectacles it can be something of a shock to discover that Christian chivalry and magnanimity were more than matched by cruelty and savagery. In 1156, Aimery, the patriarch of the Christian city of Antioch in Syria, was taken prisoner and brutally beaten around the head before having honey rubbed into his broken skin. His tormentors then chained him up outside in the full heat of the day as human fly-paper. Aimery's persecutor was not a sadistic Muslim but the Christian crusader Reynald of Châtillon, who wanted the patriarch to surrender to him his considerable wealth. Why? Because Reynald wanted to invade the rich island of Cyprus – Christian Cyprus. This he duly did, with his Armenian allies, and subjected the island to a three-week orgy of violence. As the historian Sir Steven Runciman remarked: "The murder and rapine was on a scale that the Huns or Mongols might have envied."

ABOVE *Christian knights embark for the crusades in this mid-14th-century French illumination. Among the flags on show are those of France (fleurs-de-lys), England (three lions) and the Holy See (cross keys).*

Although it must be said that Reynald was widely recognized by his fellow crusaders to be ruthless and irresponsible, even those with the noblest reputations were capable of terrible violence. Richard the Lionheart, the paragon of English chivalry, had a couple of thousand Muslim prisoners butchered in cold blood. The Christian generals besieging the Turkish-held city of Nicaea in Anatolia (modern Turkey) tried to dampen the spirits of the defenders by lobbing over the walls the hacked-off heads of dead Muslim soldiers. Yet it is well to remember that the violence of the crusades was not unusual in an age when brutal warfare was commonplace. Nor, of course, were the atrocities and cruelty one-sided – the Muslims were quite capable of matching the savagery of their Christian enemies.

Another common conception of the crusades is that it was a titanic clash of civilizations and religions, west versus east, Christianity versus Islam, inspired by idealism and dogmatic theologies. Yet as historian Jeremy Johns has written: "Christendom's assault against the Muslims had less to do with the relationship between Christianity and Islam than with the internal stresses and strains of Christian Europe." Of course it is true that the crusaders, in the main, were fired up by religious zeal and that, over time, the Muslim idea of *jihad*, that is holy war against the infidel, reasserted itself. But there were other, more secular, motives for crusading, discussed in Chapter Two. Also, from the Muslim point of view, the crusades had far less historical significance than the threat to Islam from the Mongols. In 1258 the Mongol general Hülegü destroyed a huge Muslim army before capturing the city of Baghdad, slaughtering tens of thousands of its citizens. But for a decisive riposte by the Mamluks of Egypt, the entire Muslim Middle East might have come under Mongol control.

In the early years of the twenty-first century, when conflicts in the Middle East and other parts of the world incorporate strong religious elements, it is tempting to set modern struggles in the tradition of the crusades. Indeed, the rhetoric of the crusades is sometimes drawn upon for publicity or propaganda. In 1920, a French army took over Damascus under the mandate of the League of Nations in the aftermath of World War I; its commander made his way to the tomb of Saladin – the great Muslim hero who recaptured Jerusalem from the Christians in 1187 – and declared: *"Nous revoilà, Saladin!"* ("Here we are again, Saladin!"). Saddam Hussein, the Iraqi leader who was deposed in 2003, had his portrait put on a postage stamp beside that of Saladin in an attempt to depict himself as a latter-day Muslim knight. Even the word "crusade" can raise pulses in the Muslim world, as "*jihad*" sometimes does in the west. President George W. Bush, in the aftermath of the terrorist attacks on the World Trade Center in New York on September 11, 2001, talked of mounting a "crusade" against terror, and although he was using the word in its general, non-historical meaning, it rang alarm bells in the Muslim world.

Yet to try to make facile connections between present conflicts involving Muslim and non-Muslim countries and the crusades is misleading, because it ignores the very different geo-political and religious circumstances and various other complexities. In the crusades era, for example, the Franks of the Latin east could at times live quite peacefully with their Muslim neighbours and cooperate with them over trade. (Indeed, when Prince Edward of England arrived in the Holy Land in 1271 he found that the Venetians were supplying weapons materials to his Muslim opponents!) Equally, the Christians were often drawn into conflicts among themselves – Latin Franks against Greek Byzantines, Venetians against Genoese – in the same way that the Muslims were also often caught up in internal strife. Nor was the religious element straightforward: the Catholic crusaders were generally hostile toward the Orthodox Byzantines, whom they held to be schismatics, while in the Muslim world, the orthodox Sunnis were usually at odds with the Shiites. There were also racial complexities: Christians and Muslims were not ethnically homogeneous. Those whom the Muslims bracketed under the term "Franks" actually consisted of men from France, England, Spain, Italy, Germany and other parts of Europe, among whom keen rivalries often existed. Equally, those usually labelled by the Christians as "Saracens" might be Syrians, Egyptians or Turks, who themselves could be Seljuks, Danishmends or, later on, Ottomans.

Although this book concentrates on the major expeditions to the Latin east, it is important to remember that the concept of the "crusade" was applied to theatres of war other than Outremer, for example Spain. There, for centuries, Christians fought the Moors – Muslim Arabs and Berbers who had invaded the country in 711 and conquered most of the Iberian peninsula by 718. The Christian *Reconquista* of Spain gained momentum in the late eleventh century, when Alfonso VI scored important victories against the Muslims with the help of Rodrigo Diaz, better known as El Cid, who became a national hero. It was late in the same century that the first crusade in the country was formally initiated, when in 1096 Pope Urban II encouraged Catalan crusaders bound for the Holy Land to fulfil their vows by fighting the Moors in Spain instead. Thenceforth, several crusades were launched to reinvigorate the *Reconquista*, especially after the Christian victory over the Moors at the battle of Las Navas de Tolosa in 1212. Crusading in Spain was also prominent in the early fourteenth century and the late fifteenth century until, in 1492, the last Moorish enclave of Granada fell.

It should also be stressed that crusades were not merely confined to combating Muslims. They were also launched at various times against: pagans in eastern Germany and the Baltic region; heretics, such as the Albigenses of Languedoc in the south of France and the Hussites in Bohemia; and political enemies of the pope in Italy. For what marked out a crusade was not so much the nature of the enemy but its endorsement by the pope and his granting of spiritual rewards in the form of indulgences as well as certain privileges, such as the protection of property while the crusaders were absent from home. Thus the historian Jonathan Riley-Smith has defined a crusade as "a holy war fought against those perceived to be the external or internal foes of Christendom for the recovering of Christian property or in defence of the Church or Christian people."

Nevertheless, the most glamorous, prestigious and high-profile crusades of the Middle Ages were recognized to be those against the Muslims in the east, and it is these which form the main narrative of this book, from the Council of Clermont in 1095 to the fall of Acre in 1291. *The Crusades* also sets out the historical background to the expeditions and describes the social, political and religious conditions in Outremer. Short biographies of the leading characters and a chronology are included to give signposts along what can be a tangled path of events, politics and personal names – in the index of Sir Steven Runciman's third volume of his *History of the Crusades* there are listed six different Bohemonds, 13 Baldwins and 33 Williams. It goes without saying that the modest aim of an introductory book of this nature is to encourage the reader to study more specialist works – whether those of contemporary chroniclers, such as John of Joinville, or modern studies, particularly those by Runciman and Riley-Smith – and suggestions for further reading are listed in the bibliography.

THE WORLD OF THE CRUSADES

This late-19th century map shows southeastern Europe and the Middle East, with their political boundaries, at the time of the crusades' period. The Byzantine Empire is termed the "Eastern Roman Empire" and shaded in maroon. The inset plan of Jerusalem, bottom left, marks the Church of the Holy Sepulchre and, to the right of it, the Dome of the Rock. The nearby al-Aqsa mosque, which the Knights Templar made into their headquarters, is indicated by the letter "h". The city's gates are marked by other letters of the alphabet. The inset map, top right, shows the kingdom of Jerusalem, outlined in yellow, with the main Frankish baronies (prefaced by a "B").

Other important landmarks on the map include the Byzantine capital of Constantinople ("Constantinopolis"), modern Istanbul, situated between the Sea of Marmara (unnamed) and the Black Sea ("Pontus"); Damietta, on the edge of the Nile Delta, which featured in the Fifth Crusade and the French king Louis IX's first crusade; and Tunis ("Tunes"), west of Sicily, the destination of Louis's second crusade.

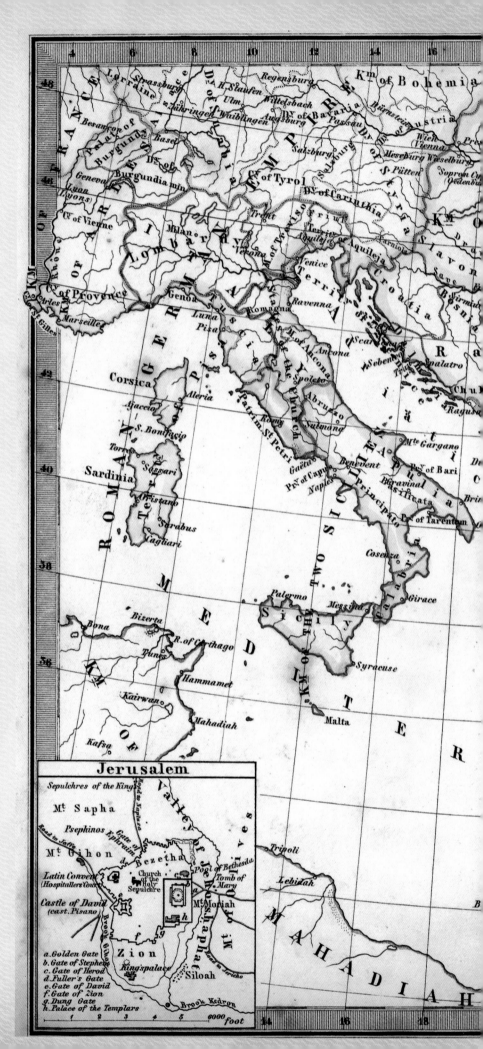

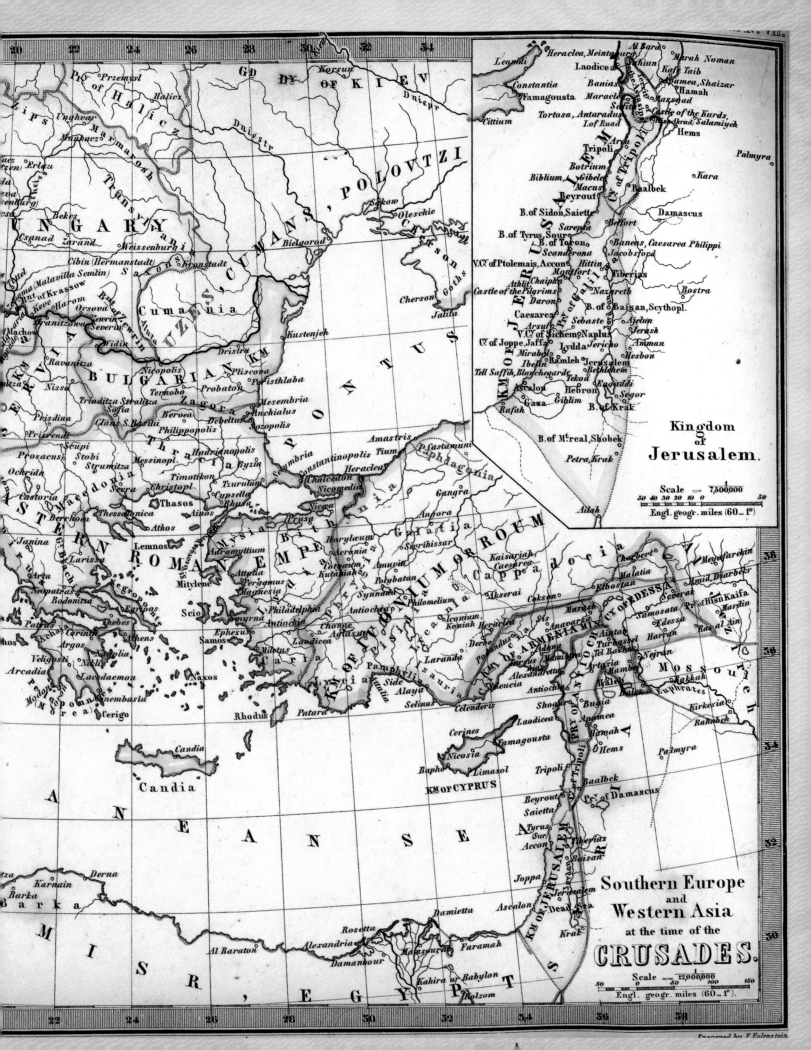

Kingdom of Jerusalem.

Scale 1 : 7,500,000

50 40 30 20 10 0   50
Engl. geogr. miles (60 = 1°)

Southern Europe and Western Asia at the time of the CRUSADES.

Scale 1 : 12,000,000

50   0   50   100   150
Engl. geogr. miles (60 = 1°).

Engraved by F. Eulenstein.

Inset map — Kingdom of Jerusalem

Al Bara, Heraclea, Meintabura, Marah Noman, Kafr Taib, Laodicea, Banias, Apamea, Shaizar, Hamah, Macus, Massad, Leonli, Constantia, Famagousta, Maracle, Tortosa, Antaradus, I.of Ruad, Castle of the Kurds, Akkrad, Salamiyeh, Cittium, Hems, Tripoli, Palmyra, Arca, Botrium, Kara, Biblium, Gibelet, Macus, Baalbek, Beyrout, B. of Sidon, Saiette, Sarepta, Belfort, Damascus, B. of Tyrus, Sour, B. of Toron, Scandrona, Buneas, Caesarea Philippi, Jacobsford, V.C. of Ptolemais, Accon, Hittin, Montfort, Tiberias, Athlit, Chaipha, Nazareth, Castle of the Pilgrims, Daron, Bostra, Caesarea, B. of Baisan, Scythopl., Arsur, Sebaste, Ajelun, V.C. of Sichem, Naplus, Jerash, Cy. of Joppe, Jaffa, Lydda, Jericho, Amman, Mirabel, Hesbon, Ibelin, Ramleh, Jerusalem, Tell Saffik, Blanchegarde, Tekoa, Eugaldi, Ascalon, Hebron, Segor, Gaza, Giblim, B. of Krak, Rafah, B. of M.real, Shobek, Petra, Krak, Ailah

Main map labels

P.ty of Halicz, Przemysl, Haliez, Unghvar, Marmarosh, Munkacz, Zips, Erlau, Transylvania, GD DY OF KIEV, Korsun, Dniepr, Dniestr, CUMANS, POLOVTZI, Sekow, Oleschie, Bielgorod, UNGARY, Bekes, Csanad, Zarand, Weissenburg, Cibin (Hermanstadt), Saxons, Kronstadt, Cherson, Tyttel, Malavilla, Semlin, B.t of Krassow, Kese, Harom, Orsova, Severin, Branitzowa, Cumania, UZEN, Aluta, Widin, Machow, SERVIA, Ravanitza, Nicopolis, KM, Dristra, Kustenjeh, Nissa, BULGARIAN, Pliscova, Prisdina, Ternobo, Probaton, Poristhlaba, Prisrendi, Triaditza, Straliza, Zagora, Mesembria, PONTUS, Sofia, Beroea, Debeltus, Anchialus, Claus, S.Basilii, Philippopolis, Sozopolis, Prosacus, Scupi, Stobi, Hadrianopolis, Amastris, P.Castamuni, Paphlagonia, Ochrida, Strumitza, Thracia, Selumbria, Byzia, Tium, Castoria, Berrhoea, Messinopl, Timotikon, Tzurulum, Constantinopolis, Heraclea, Gangra, Macedonia, Sera, Christopl, Typsella, Rhusa, Chalcedon, Nicaea, Prusa, Janina, Larissa, Thasos, Ainos, Nicomedia, Ancora, Galatia, Arta, Neopatras, Lemnos, Mysia, Adramyttium, Bithynia, Dorylaeum, Acrania, Sivrihissar, Kaisariah, Caesarea, Cappadocia, Rozbert, Megafarekin, Bodonitza, Euboea, Attalia, Pergamus, Magnesia, Kutahiah, Amuria, Polybaton, Philomelium, Akserai, Cokson, Malatia, Elbostan, Amid, Diarbekr, P.ty of Hisn Kaifa, Mardin, Thebes, Scio, Philadelphia, Smyrna, Antiochia, Chonae, Agiasun, Laodicea, Iconium, Koniah, Heraclea, Sis, Anavarsa, Aintab, Turbassel, Samosata, Edessa, Ras al Ain, Patras, Achaia, Corinth, Athens, Ephesus, Milutus, Carra, Derbe, Podandus, Larenda, KM OF ARMENIA, Adana, Mamistra, Tel Bashir, Nejran, Veligosti, Nicli, Nauplia, Samos, Pamphylia, Satalia, Isauria, Tarsus, Alexandretta, Ayas, Artesia, Mambeg, Mossoul, Arcadia, Lacedaemon, Side, Alaya, Seleucia, Antiochia, Py of Antioch, Haleb, Bales, Euphrates, Kirkesia, Rahabeh, Modon, Monembasia, Cerigo, Rhodus, Patara, Selinus, Celenderis, Shogur, Bugia, Apamea, Naxos, Laodicea, Cerines, Famagousta, Hamah, Hems, Palmyra, Bapho, Nicosia, Limasol, KM OF CYPRUS, Tripoli, Py of Tripoli, Baalbek, Candia, Beyrout, Py of Damascus, Saietta, Tyrus, Sur, Accon, Tiberias, Baisan, Joppa, Jerusalem, KM OF JERUSALEM, Dead Sea, Ascalon, Krak, Derna, Karnain, Barka, MISR, EGYPT, Rosetta, Alexandria, Damietta, Al Baraton, Damanhour, Mansura, Faramah, Kahira or Babylon, Holzom, MEDITERRANEAN SEA, AEGEAN SEA, EASTERN ROMAN EMPIRE

THE HOLY LAND

The start of the crusading movement and the course it took in the east was to some extent influenced by historical events that occurred hundreds of years before Pope Urban II preached the First Crusade in 1095. Many questions are raised by the crusades: for example, how did the Holy Land gain a mystique in the Christian imagination and how were the crusades connected with pilgrimage (crusaders saw themselves as pilgrims, albeit armed ones intent on conquest, and would perform religious rituals associated with pilgrimages)?

Why were western crusaders chronically suspicious of, and hostile to, their fellow Christians in Byzantium (and vice versa)? How did religious and political differences between Muslims play into the hands of the crusaders?

To answer these questions it is necessary to go back to the early centuries AD and trace the development of the church within the context of the Roman Empire and the rise and consolidation of Islam.

THE EARLY CHURCH

By the start of the fourth century AD, the Roman Empire was divided in two parts, western and eastern, each ruled by an emperor and his deputy. At this time, Roman citizens were predominantly pagans, although a sizeable number of Christians were living in various parts of the empire as an occasionally persecuted minority. The political and religious map of the empire changed, however, with the coming to power of the Roman general Constantine as emperor of the west. According to tradition, Constantine received a vision of the cross before the battle against his rival Maxentius that would bring him to power in 312. He interpreted this as a positive Christian symbol, and after his victory he made the Christian faith the most favoured in the empire. Clergymen were excused having to pay taxes; Sunday became a holiday; the church was allowed to inherit property by law; and celibacy was no longer a target for financial penalties. Constantine had

ABOVE The city of Jerusalem, depicted in this painting by the 19th-century British painter David Roberts, became a goal for increasing numbers of Christian pilgrims from the fourth century onward.

imposing churches built and in 330 – six years after he had also become emperor of the eastern Roman Empire – he turned the old Greek settlement of Byzantium on the Bosphorus, at the crossroads of Europe and Asia, into his new eastern capital of Constantinople. So now there were two capitals of the Roman Empire: Rome in the west, and Constantinople – the "new Rome" – in the east. After Constantine died in 337, almost all his Roman imperial successors continued to support the church, and by the end of the fourth century Emperor Theodosius I had outlawed pagan rituals, was destroying pagan temples and punishing Christian heretics.

It was from the time of Constantine onward that Jerusalem and the other holy sites of Palestine became an increasing attraction for Christian pilgrims. This phenomenon owed much to Constantine's mother, Helena, a devoted Christian who, in 326, embarked for the Holy Land when she was in her late 70s. According to pious legend, during excavations of Jesus' tomb in Jerusalem, she discovered the True Cross, the one, that is, on which he had been crucified. Part of the cross was kept in Jerusalem, while a section was sent off to Constantinople. It was not long before hundreds of minute fragments of the cross were circulating around Christendom. (In crusading times, the portion of the True Cross in Jerusalem was captured by the Muslims at the battle of Hattin in 1187 and never returned to Christian ownership.)

Constantine and Helena also initiated a substantial building programme in Palestine, the most important edifice of which was the Church of the Holy Sepulchre, which stood on the places where, by tradition, Jesus was executed and buried. If Jerusalem was the centre of the Christian cosmos, then the Holy Sepulchre was the spiritual centre of Jerusalem, the most sacred spot in Christendom. (Not surprisingly, the crusader kings of Jerusalem chose it for their burial place – although their bones were exhumed and scattered by the Khwarazmian Turks after they captured Jerusalem in 1244.) When pilgrims and crusaders first arrived in Jerusalem the Holy Sepulchre was invariably their first port of call and typically induced great outpourings of emotion. The church itself originally comprised a complex of buildings that included a domed structure raised over Christ's tomb and, separate from it, a large, richly carved and gilded basilica. In the following centuries the church was twice destroyed and rebuilt; then in the 1140s the crusaders redesigned it so that its different elements were united under one roof.

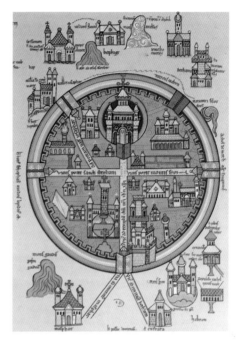

ABOVE *This facsimile of a medieval map of Jerusalem shows the city schematically divided into four parts within a circular wall. The Dome of the Rock, depicted as the Temple of Solomon, is featured at top.*

THE CALL OF THE HOLY LAND

But it was not just the memorials to Jesus' death and resurrection, potent though they were, which brought visitors to the Holy Land. One of the first western pilgrims to reach Palestine was the anonymous Bordeaux pilgrim in 333–34. This man (or possibly woman) took the route that the armies of the First Crusade and other subsequent expeditions followed, namely overland through the Balkans to Constantinople (modern Istanbul) then south through Anatolia (modern Turkey) and Syria to Jerusalem – a journey of some 3,250 miles (5,250 km). In Jerusalem, apart from the Holy Sepulchre, the pilgrim was shown the column against which Jesus was whipped; the "pinnacle of the Temple", from which the devil tried to tempt Jesus to throw himself; and even the palm tree whose branches were cut to line the path of Jesus during his triumphal entry into Jerusalem. He also visited the nearby village of Bethany, the home of Mary and Martha and their brother Lazarus, whom Jesus brought back from the dead; the ruins of the city of Jericho; and the Dead Sea.

It is clear that by the time of the Bordeaux pilgrim a number of sites in Palestine, and not just Jerusalem, were regarded by Christians as sacred places. This sense of sanctity was later consolidated by St Jerome (c. 342–420), who is probably best known for translating the Bible into the Latin text known as the Vulgate. Through his spiritual standing, his letters and other writings, Jerome was important for developing the idea of the Holy Land as a pilgrimage destination (he himself settled and ended his days in Bethlehem), as well as for the Christian tradition of the veneration of relics (see Box, p. 18). In one of his letters, written to a Roman widow named Marcella on behalf of friends of his, Jerome argues that a visit to Jerusalem was the best way of rounding off a Christian's spiritual

HOLY RELICS

One of the principal motives for making a pilgrimage in medieval times was to see, and if possible touch, one or more holy relics. These were usually the remains of a saint whose intercessions with God on behalf of the supplicant might succeed in effecting a cure or bringing good luck. The crusaders, like any other pilgrims, were keen to acquire relics. When King Andrew of Hungary, for instance, returned home from Outremer in January 1218, he was laden with relics, including the head of St Stephen, the first Christian martyr, and one of the jugs that held the water which Jesus turned to wine during the wedding feast at Cana. The crusaders' sack and looting of Constantinople in 1204 resulted in a flood of relics reaching the west – one Latin monk is said to have stolen an array of relics that included a fragment of the True Cross, the arm of St James, a tooth of St Lawrence, and a foot of St Cosmas. Another sliver of the True Cross reached the priory of Bromholm in eastern England in 1223 and was immediately reported to have miraculous healing powers, instantly making the priory an important pilgrimage centre.

The church's high regard for relics went back to the early years of its history, and by early medieval times they had become standard items in worship. In 787 the Second Council of Nicaea decreed that no church could be consecrated without possessing a relic. As the church expanded during the crusading period, relics were brought back to Europe from the Holy Land to meet the ever-increasing demand.

Over time, some relics gained more prestige than others, for example the skulls of the three Magi at Cologne, the remains of St James at Santiago de Compostela in Spain, and the remains of St Peter and St Paul at Rome. Less well known are the tens of thousands of other relics that were kept in Europe's churches and shrines, whether splinters from the True Cross or the bones, teeth, hair and nail clippings of countless saints. Relics were usually preserved in beautifully worked reliquaries, ranging from gold-plated, gem-studded chests to gilt arm-shaped cases enclosing the arm bones of saints and small pendants holding locks of saints' hair. Reliquaries were displayed or carried in procession on special occasions, such as feast days, and were designed to inspire awe in onlookers.

ABOVE *This reliquary - a small 12th-century chest from Limoges, France - is made of gilded copper with enamel insertions.*

education. He also conveys the idea of a spiritual energy radiating out from the Holy Land, attracting pilgrims to Jerusalem from all over the empire, including from Gaul, Britain, Armenia, Persia, India, Arabia, Egypt and elsewhere. The letter ends with a list of the Palestinian sites that by this time were on the pilgrims' trail, including Nazareth; Cana, where Jesus turned water into wine at a wedding feast; Nain, where he raised a widow's son from the dead; Capernaum in Galilee; Mount Tabor, where he was transfigured by a divine light; and the River Jordan.

ABOVE *This aerial view of Jerusalem is taken from the southwest and looks across the city to the Dome of the Rock. The Tower of the Ascension can be seen top right.*

THE BARBARIAN INVASIONS

L iving in a cell in Bethlehem, Jerome lived long enough to hear about the sack of Rome, the Eternal City, in 410 by the barbarian Visigoths. It was an event that contemporaries found hard to comprehend, and one that was a significant landmark in the protracted decline and fall of the western Roman Empire. Why this happened is still a matter of debate, with poor government, economic depression and poor morale in the armed forces all playing their part. Whatever the reasons, Germanic tribes such as the Goths, Franks and Vandals infiltrated imperial territories and by the early 500s had created independent kingdoms. However, these so-called barbarians – some of them already half-Romanized and most of them Christians, albeit mainly of the heretical Arian variety – were not totally destructive and gradually absorbed and preserved some of the old Roman customs and culture. And although the central government in Italy was no longer presided over by a Roman emperor, the Roman church, through the actions of vigorous popes such as Leo I (d. 461) and Gregory I, the Great (590–604), maintained its spiritual leadership in the west.

Whereas the western Roman Empire had fallen to the Germanic invaders, the eastern Roman Empire, centred on Constantinople, survived and gradually became known as the Byzantine Empire, after the original name of its capital. Indeed, now that Constantinople was the seat of the sole remaining Roman emperor, its prestige rose; and its bishop, known as the patriarch, became Christianity's second most important prelate after the pope. During the sixth century, the Byzantines mounted a counterattack against the Germanic barbarians in the west, invading Africa, Spain, and northern Italy, with some success. But in the east in the following century, they had to face a new adversary that had suddenly burst onto the political scene and would eventually, in centuries to come, preside over their destruction.

ISLAM TRIUMPHANT

The rise of Islam was sudden and explosive. The religion was founded by the Prophet Muhammad, a trader from Mecca who experienced divine revelations, and, after his death in 632, it spread rapidly from Arabia. The first victims of Muslim expansion were the Byzantines and the Persians, the two great regional powers who had exhausted themselves fighting each other and were in no fit state to repel the new menace that confronted them. Filled with religious zeal and confidence, the swift, disciplined Muslim Arab cavalry won victory after victory. They swept north into Palestine, taking Jerusalem in 638 (and behaving with great restraint, in contrast to the crusaders' butchery on regaining the holy city in 1099) and Syria and eastern Anatolia. In the east they conquered Iran, and in the west they advanced along the North African coast to what is now Morocco. From there, in 711, a Muslim Arab and Berber army invaded Spain and proceeded to conquer most of the country. By 720 they had crossed the Pyrenees and were pushing into France, and only a crushing defeat in 732 at Poitiers at the hands of the Franks under Charles Martel stopped their further advance. In less than a century after Muhammad's death, Islam, led by the Umayyad dynasty, stretched from the borders of China to the Atlantic Ocean (see Box, p. 20).

Despite Muslim domination of Palestine, Christian pilgrims were able to visit the holy sites in Jerusalem and elsewhere without too much trouble until the eleventh century. Visitors did need official passes and a certain amount of ready cash to bribe or tip the local Muslim bureaucrats, but on the whole it seems that Christians were able to move around unhindered. The great Frankish king Charlemagne, who became Holy Roman Emperor in the west in 800, improved the lot of Christian travellers to Jerusalem by having a pilgrims' hostel built in the city. He was able to do this partly because of the good diplomatic relationship he enjoyed with the Abbasid caliph Harun ar-Rashid. (Indeed, cordial relations between Christian and Muslim nobles would also occasionally surface during the period of the crusades: the friendship between Richard the Lionheart and the brother of his adversary Saladin, and the mutual fascination between Emperor Frederick II and Sultan al-Kamil are two such examples.)

The good understanding between the Muslim authorities and Christian pilgrims broke down in the early eleventh century, however, during the regime of Hakim, the Fatimid caliph of Egypt, who suddenly ordered the destruction of the Holy Sepulchre and the persecution of Christians. The situation improved after Hakim's death in 1021, and in the following years large groups of Christians continued to make their way to Palestine. In 1026 a band of 700 pilgrims, subsidized by Richard II, duke of Normandy, travelled to the Holy Land. And in 1065, more than 12,000 German pilgrims – a veritable army – under the bishop of Bamberg arrived there too.

CHRISTENDOM DISUNITED

But problems again arose for Christian pilgrims after the rise of the Seljuk Turks. In 1070, the Seljuks, already by this time the effective power behind the Abbasid caliphate in Baghdad, captured Jerusalem from the Fatimid dynasty of Egypt. Then in the following year they routed the Byzantine army at Manzikert in Armenia – a decisive victory that enabled them to dominate Anatolia

SUNNIS, SHIITES AND MUSLIM DYNASTIES

The Muslim world that the crusaders entered was not homogeneous either in ethnicity or religion. For example, although the first Muslim armies were at first composed mainly of Arabs, by about 700 onward Persians, Turks, North African Berbers and others who had been converted to Islam were increasingly used. And in matters of religion there was a fundamental divide between two major groups: Sunnis and Shiites. The tension between the two sides was deeply rooted and, in crusader times, contributed to the complex and habitually fractious nature of Muslim politics in the Near East, often to the advantage of the Christian settlers.

The Sunnis, the "followers of the tradition", who comprised the majority of Muslims, regarded themselves as mainstream orthodox believers, as they still do. The Shiites hold that the religious heads, or imams, of the Muslim community can only be descendants of Ali – the Prophet Muhammad's son-in-law – who was the fourth caliph, or "successor", after the death of the Prophet in 632. From the Shiite movement emerged various other groups, including the Twelvers and the Seveners. Twelver Shiites acknowledge the authority of only the first 12 imams in the line of descent from Ali. They believe that the last of them, Imam al-Mahdi, disappeared in 874 according to God's plan but that he is still alive and will return in the future to lead his followers to victory and inaugurate the Last Judgment. Seveners are also called Ismailis because in 765 they backed a man named Ismail over another claimant to be the seventh imam of the Shiites.

The first great Muslim dynasty was the Umayyads, whose caliphs reigned from 661 to 750 and continued the initial spectacular expansion of Islam from its Arabian heartland that took place under the first four caliphs. Based in Damascus, the Umayyads pursued the policy of allowing Jews and Christians, whom Muslims regarded as People of the Book, to practise their religion, subject to paying a poll tax. They were also patrons of art and architecture. Under Caliph Abd al-Malik, the holy shrine of the Dome of the Rock – whose golden cupola still shines out over Jerusalem – was built in 691 on the site of the Jewish Temple.

The Umayyads were succeeded by the Abbasids, who reigned from 750 to 1258 – well into the crusades era – and moved the caliphate to Baghdad. From about the middle of the eleventh century, however, the Abbasids were effectively puppets of the Seljuk Turks, a nomadic tribe who had been serving them as soldiers. Although the Seljuks maintained the Abbasid caliphs as figureheads and upheld the Sunni tradition, it was their own sultans who held the real power, backed up by a powerful military force; and it was the Seljuks who would prove to be the crusaders' first Muslim adversaries in Anatolia.

The weakness of Abbasid rule from the tenth century onward saw the rise of independent Muslim kingdoms in various parts of the empire. One of the most important of these was the Fatimid dynasty in Egypt (909–1171), who founded an Ismaili, or Sevener, Shiite caliphate – based in their newly built city of Cairo – which rivalled the Sunni caliphate of the Abbasids. The Fatimids were succeeded in Egypt and other parts of the Near East by the Ayubid dynasty, established by the greatest of Muslim generals, Saladin. He and his successors held sway until the rise to power in the mid-thirteenth century of the last great Muslim dynasty to face the crusaders in the Latin east, the Mamluks of Egypt. The Mamluks were originally slaves who had been converted to Islam and trained to serve as crack troops under the Fatimid caliphs. It was the Mamluks who eventually presided over the final destruction of the crusader settlements in 1291.

RIGHT *Shiite martyrs killed in battle fighting against their fellow Muslims during the 7th century are laid out on the ground in this 17th-century mural from Isfahan in Iran.*

and soon reduce Byzantine territory to a small area around Constantinople. The Seljuk threat prompted the Byzantine emperor, Alexius I Comnenus, to send envoys to the Council of Piacenza in March 1095, requesting help from Pope Urban II – what they said is not certain, but they probably painted a lurid picture of potential Muslim domination in the east.

In fact, although Alexius and Urban were on relatively good terms, the Roman Catholic Church and the Greek Orthodox Church had been in a state of formal schism since a dramatic contretemps between the two sides in 1054. The quarrel was symptomatic of differences that had been brewing for centuries. The papacy, which had originally looked toward the Byzantine emperors for support, had been distancing itself from them since the 700s, when Pope Stephen II followed by Pope Leo III, had instead looked westward to the kings of the Franks as political protectors. There were also various divergences between the churches over doctrine and customs (for example the Greeks fasted on Saturdays, whereas the Latins did not). And the outlook of each church toward the other was underpinned by general cultural differences between the Latin west and Greek east that were to harden into prejudices. Westerners tended to caricature the Byzantines as weak, effeminate, manipulative and treacherous schismatics, whereas to the Byzantines, most westerners seemed to be uncultured, boorish, arrogant and over-aggressive. During much of the period of the crusades there was little love lost between the two major branches of Christendom, and their inability to pull together in a common cause was constantly deleterious to the Christian campaign in the Latin east, or Outremer. When finally, in 1204, the Fourth Crusade was directed at Constantinople and not the Holy Land it brought the chronic antagonism between Christian east and west to a catastrophic head.

Nevertheless, despite the generally strained relations between the two churches, Urban responded to Alexius's request in the most positive fashion – indeed, Urban may have been considering sending help to the Byzantines six years previously. The pope had hopes that a western task force might not only save the Byzantine Empire and the holy places of Palestine but also lead to a reunification of the churches under papal leadership. What Alexius probably wanted was just a small band of mercenaries to help him roll back Seljuk gains in Anatolia. What he received was a vast, barely controllable host, intent on rescuing the Holy Land from the infidel.

et austres sains lieux la enuiron. Et les ypiens yhabitans z demou rans. z que les austres par eulx tyranniquement z Inhumaine ment tues. Ils auoient reseruc en Inseruitude vie a fin que sur eulx en lopprobre du sainct nom ypieu prissent continuer plus longuement leurs Insatiables miulites. Et comment Ils les tenoient en trop opprobrieuse captiuite z seruage. ou tresgrant deshoneur z opprobre de tous les ypiens. Concluant z mon strant par diuerses raisons tres euidentes que le sainct peuple ypieu ne debuoit plus souffri nendurer que les sains lieux et

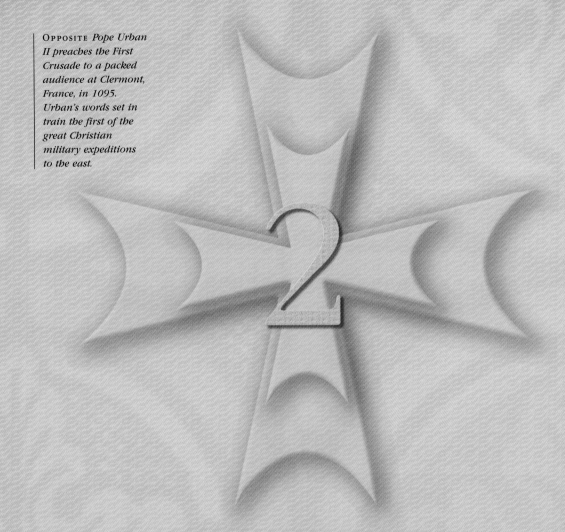

"GOD WILLS IT!"

The Chinese sage Laozi once remarked that even the longest journey begins with a short step. The short step from which the epic Christian crusading enterprise in the Middle East proceeded was taken by Pope Urban II at the Council of Clermont in the Massif Central region of France, on November 27, 1095. According to the medieval chroniclers, most of them writing some time after the event, Urban gave a speech that lit the fuse to an explosive keg of religious aspirations and aggression, mixed with fantasies of power and booty, which was subsequently channelled through a succession of Christian expeditions to the east. The immediate result was the First Crusade, the capture of Jerusalem and the foundation of crusader settlements in the Holy Land that would survive for nearly 200 years. What was it Urban said to make such an impact?

THE CALL TO ARMS

The pope's speech, as reported by the chroniclers, was an event of pure drama – perhaps carefully orchestrated, since it seems that the idea for a crusade had already been broached by Urban before Clermont. Opening on November 18, the council at first proceeded mundanely. Various church matters were attended to, with decrees issued about, among other things, clergy conducting burials free of charge, people fasting between Ash Wednesday and Easter, and the reaffirmation of the church-inspired Truce of God – the suspension of warfare at certain times of the year. Toward the end of the proceedings, however, Urban spread the word that he was going to make a special announcement on the 27th.

On that day, anticipatory excitement drew such great crowds that the pope had to set up a platform in the fields outside the city walls. There are a number of versions of what Urban said, none of them verbatim accounts, but the gist is that he told a rapt audience that the Byzantines had requested aid in the face of attacks by the Turks. With grand rhetorical flourishes he spoke of Christians being killed, enslaved, raped and forcibly converted to Islam and churches being destroyed (although in fact the Turkish advance in Anatolia had stalled by 1092). He then turned to the remedy: Christians of the west must rally to help their eastern brothers and free Christ's tomb in the Church of the Holy Sepulchre in Jerusalem from the Muslim yoke. Instead of engaging in fratricidal warfare at home, they should shed the blood of the infidel abroad, in the name of God, who would ensure victory. As Urban's voice boomed across the fields, the response was spontaneous and electrifying: cries of *Deus le Volt!* ("God wills it!") rose from the cheering crowd. Adhémar, the bishop of Le Puy, implored the pope on bent knees to be allowed to participate in the rescue mission, and there and then hundreds of others followed suit.

Urban's speech at Clermont was like a fountain of pure enthusiasm, its spray wafting over France, the main target of the pope's appeal, and other parts of western Europe. His words and subsequent recruiting drives over the following months touched the minds and hearts not only of the west's nobility and finest fighting men – indeed it was the latter Urban had specifically in mind when making his appeal – but also the poor and outcasts of society. As priests and monks preached the holy war in their local regions, Urban's call to arms began to materialize in the practical preparations that would soon send vast armies eastward.

THE CRUSADING SPIRIT

There has been much scholarly ink spilled over what exactly drove so many thousands of ordinary men and women to endure terrible hardships and risk their lives in such a dangerous enterprise. Certainly, in an age of widespread religious piety, when endowments to the church were readily made, spiritual idealism was a major, if not the premier, reason. Jerusalem and the Holy Land had been the most sacred Christian pilgrimage destination for centuries. In the imagination of many, the walls, towers, gates and shrines of the terrestrial Jerusalem somehow merged with the heavenly Jerusalem of the Book of Revelation, which shone "with the glory of God, and its brilliance was like that of a very precious jewel, like a jasper, clear as crystal ... The twelve gates were twelve pearls ... The great street of the city was of pure gold, like transparent glass" (21:11, 21). To Christians, Jerusalem was reckoned to be the centre of the world, and the heart of Jerusalem was the Church of the Holy Sepulchre, the most holy and evocative spot in Christendom. To free the land where Jesus and his disciples lived and died from the infidel could easily be seen as a sacred duty. Indeed, to contemporaries, the layman's participation in a crusade was as meritorious as becoming a monk.

There were also less spiritual motives for going on crusade. It fulfilled the widespread desire among those belonging to the upper echelons of society for adventure and glory through fighting. The Peace of God movement, instigated by the influential abbey of Cluny in the late tenth century, and later the Truce of God movement had sought to restrain the martial instincts of hot-headed aristocrats. Now the latter had the chance to channel their lust for battle in a way that honoured God – the pope, acting on behalf of the church, was legitimizing their undoubted flair for killing. Over time, from at least the Fourth Crusade (1204), crusading became an important part of the romantic mystique of the knight, an ideal of chivalric behaviour.

Material benefits were also part of the crusades' attraction. They offered those who for one reason or another found themselves landless or destitute at home the chance to enjoy a higher standard of living in the east. Like the first European colonists in the New World, many crusaders were simply looking for a better life. However, it should be emphasized that most nobles envisaged the crusade as a "tour of duty" and looked forward to their return home. Also, the idea that crusading was a sort of California Gold Rush for the impecunious younger sons of aristocrats is now widely rejected; far from making huge fortunes, most knights incurred expenses – to pay for horses, pack-animals, weapons, armour and servants – that outweighed their gains. Most important of all, perhaps, the crusades offered the chance of reaching paradise. At Clermont, Urban had promised the full remission of sins to those who took the cross. In a world where the idea of hell or purgatory with all their terrible tortures loomed large and the consciousness of one's sins was intense, the idea that the crusades' tortuous journeys would cancel out all penance owed to God was an extraordinary boon (see Box).

THE PEOPLE'S CRUSADE

The First Crusade broadly consisted of two expeditions. The so-called People's Crusade seems to have consisted of an array of peasants, some townsfolk, and a mixture of brigands, ruffians

ABOVE *Horned devils thrust the souls of the damned into the mouth of a monster in a scene depicting hell from a 13th-century stained glass window from Bourges in France.*

HELL, HEAVEN & PURGATORY

What happened after death and the prospect of hell, heaven or purgatory was a constant source of speculation and anxiety to the people of the Middle Ages. It was commonly believed that the deceased went to hell if they had died unrepentant, heaven if they were saintly, and purgatory if they fell between the latter two categories. Most people anticipated an extended and unpleasant stay in purgatory, where, as St Thomas Aquinas asserted, its fiery torments were far greater than any pain suffered on earth.

The idea of purgatory hinged on the inevitability of unfulfilled penance (the word comes from the Latin for "punishment"). Priests could absolve repentant sinners of guilt, but they were still required to do penance, such as go on a fast. Yet it was a fact of life that people died before getting the chance to do the requisite penance for their sins. What happened to them? The answer was that they were condemned to a process of gruelling purification in purgatory. But it was a fate that could be shortened if the living prayed or said masses for them.

The system of penance also gave rise to the idea of indulgences. The church came to appreciate that some penances, such as long pilgrimage, were potentially disruptive to society (crucial tasks such as harvesting could be neglected) and it allowed them to be commuted to substitutes, such as flogging or a fine. This idea of indulgences, of substitutionary acts, began to crystallize from the late eleventh century into a system whereby certain pious actions were assigned specific values: for example a pilgrimage to Rome to view the holy relic known as the "Veronica" was worth 12,000 years off purgatory. There were also plenary indulgences, which offered a complete remission of penance. When Urban II issued the first of these at Clermont in 1095 it was not entirely clear whether he intended remission of all penance required to be done by repentant sinners on earth, or in purgatory. It seems certain, however, that those who eagerly took up the cross believed it to be the latter — that, in other words, they would bypass the torments of purgatory and go straight to heaven.

and vagabonds, but also, it should be noted, a significant sprinkling of knights. This was followed shortly by another sizeable force of fighting men, knights and footsoldiers whose leaders were some of the most important magnates in Europe.

The chief instigator of the People's Crusade was an itinerant French monk known as Peter the Hermit, who looked like a dirty barefoot ragamuffin but had tremendous charisma and rhetorical power. In the words of Sir Steven Runciman, Peter was "a man of short stature, swarthy and with a long lean face, horribly like the donkey that he always rode and which was revered almost as much as himself." Through force of personality and a hectic tour of preaching the crusade, Peter attracted close followers who in turn spread the word about the expedition. For the poor and dispossessed, ground down by social injustices and natural disasters (flooding and plague in 1094, drought and famine the following year), the words of Peter and his associates must have opened up the golden vista of a possible new life, and thousands began to make preparations to set out for the east.

ABOVE *Peter the Hermit, the main instigator of the People's Crusade, points the way to Jerusalem in this 14th-century illumination. Peter led his motley assortment of crusaders to disaster in Anatolia.*

In April 1096, Peter arrived in Cologne at the head of his alarming rag-tag army. There he paused and tried to recruit Germans to the cross. But his impetuous colleague, the Frenchman Walter Sans-Avoir, pressed on with the eastward march with a contingent of several thousand of his compatriots. Following the Rhine and then the Danube rivers, the French crossed into Hungary, where King Coloman helped them on their way. But when they passed into Byzantine lands near Belgrade, a shortage of food led to pillaging, which in turn led to clashes with the local Byzantine governor and his troops. Tension was defused only when Walter hurried his men to the town of Nish, south-east of Belgrade, where food was made available, and thence to Constantinople.

In time, following Walter, Peter the Hermit himself and the main body of the army of about 20,000 men marched eastward. Despite clashes with the Hungarians and, later, Byzantine troops, Peter reached Constantinople safely and was welcomed by Emperor Alexius. But to keep these rough westerners from scavenging in the local countryside, Alexius quickly shipped Peter's crusaders over the Bosphorus to a military camp named Civetot on August 6, where Walter Sans-Avoir and his men joined them.

Now that the crusaders had arrived in Asia, they had to ponder their next step. It was a mark of Peter's waning authority over his unruly troops that advice passed on to him from Alexius not to proceed farther without reinforcements from the west was widely ignored. Contingents of Germans, Italians and French, eager for food and booty, began to raid the surrounding countryside, heedless of whether their peasant victims were native Christians or Muslim Turks. In September 1096 a French force even got as far as Nicaea – the major Seljuk city of the area, lying 50 miles (80 km) south of Constantinople – and sacked its suburbs, before fighting off the city guard. Then, in a spirit of rivalry, German and Italian crusaders advanced beyond Nicaea and occupied the castle of Xerigordion, hoping to use it as a base for scavenging operations. But they were besieged there by a Turkish force, who simply waited until the Christians were maddened by thirst (they were reduced to drinking horses' blood and human urine) and forced to surrender. The lives of those few who agreed to convert to Islam were spared, but everyone else was put to death.

"GOD WILLS IT!"

ABOVE *Crusaders under Peter the Hermit are attacked and destroyed by the Seljuk Turks near the city of Nicaea in Anatolia in this 15th-century French illumination.*

THE JEWISH MASSACRES

While Peter the Hermit and his army were marching to Constantinople, back in the west three of his associates, a priest called Gottschalk, a preacher called Volksmar, and Count Emich of Leiningen were still raising small armies to join the main force. They and their troops were to become infamous, however, not for killing Muslims but for murdering Jews, whom they considered to be an enemy much closer to home. Jewish communities had existed in Europe for hundreds of years and had formed close-knit neighbourhoods in many cities, where they were valued as artisans, physicians and moneylenders (especially since Christians were banned from being usurers by the Roman Catholic Church). Yet anti-semitism in Christian societies was never far from the surface. As crusading rhetoric stirred the hearts of Christians, for many the idea of revenge being exacted on the Muslims for occupying the Holy Land could easily be transferred onto the Jews for what was widely seen as their infamous role in Christian history as "Christ-killers". There was also the motive of money; the booty taken from Jewish victims was one way of financing an expensive expedition.

Emich of Leiningen was the first to direct his force's bloodlust on a Jewish community, attacking the Jews of Speyer in Germany on May 3, 1096. Two weeks later he moved to Worms and butchered 500 men, women and children, ignoring the fact that they had taken sanctuary in the bishop's palace at the prelate's behest. A few days later it was the turn of Mainz, where thousands were killed over two days. Then at Cologne the crusaders burnt a synagogue but were prevented from wholesale massacring by the archbishop.

Meanwhile, Volksmar and his army, *en route* to the east, stopped off in Prague and began slaughtering Jews, despite the protests of the city authorities. But Volksmar's outrages ended in Hungary, where King Coloman's troops, faced with what seemed to be a dangerous, unruly mob, attacked and dispersed the crusaders, who were never heard of again.

The final member of this unholy triumvirate, Gottschalk, carried out a pogrom on the Jews of the city of Ratisbon (Regensburg) before advancing into Hungary. At first Coloman treated this latest army with respect – until the westerners began marauding and fighting the local peasants. His patience tried beyond endurance, Coloman ordered his army to teach the crusaders a fatal lesson, and no one, including Gottschalk, escaped the ensuing massacre.

The news of this setback – the first crusader defeat at the hands of the Turks – was greeted with dismay back at Civetot. The crusaders then learned that a Turkish force was advancing toward them, so their leaders, except for Peter, who was meeting the emperor in Constantinople, quickly debated what to do. Some advocated a defensive strategy, but it was those who urged that offensive action was the best policy who won the argument. On October 21, the crusader army set out to meet the enemy, promptly fell into a carefully planned ambush in a nearby valley, and was cut down by showers of arrows and a massed Turkish assault. Those who survived the onslaught fled back to Civetot, pursued hot-foot by their adversaries, who wreaked carnage in the camp, slaughtering men, women and children. A couple of thousand Christians managed to escape to a deserted castle on the coast, and there they were rescued by a Byzantine flotilla, but the aspirations of the first wave of crusaders had been bloodily dashed.

THE CRUSADER PRINCES

After a second wave of the People's Crusade ended in disaster – the crusaders' unruly violence was mostly channelled into massacring Jews in Europe (see Box) – it was the turn of some of Europe's finest princes to enter the chapters of history. They included: Hugh of Vermandois, brother of the French king and notable more for his eloquence and good looks than his fighting ability; Godfrey of Bouillon, duke of Lower Lorraine, whose mop of blond hair and imposing physique belied his average martial prowess; Godfrey's more extrovert and aggressive brother, Baldwin of Boulogne; Raymond IV of Saint-Gilles, count of Toulouse, an experienced soldier of nearly 60 years of age, who, with some justice, considered himself to be the natural lay leader of the expedition (which was in fact under papal control through the person of Adhémar, bishop of Le Puy). Then there were the formidable Norman warriors of southern Italy, Bohemond of Taranto – whose height, build and haughtiness so impressed the Byzantine emperor's

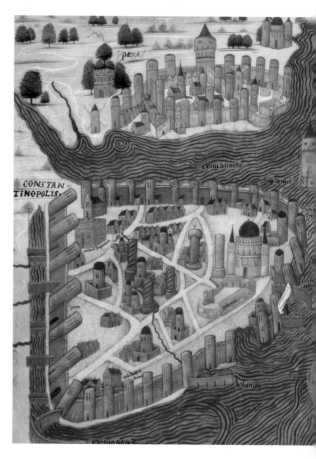

daughter, Anna Comnena – and his nephew Tancred.

The first of these crusaders to make the momentous journey to the east was Hugh of Vermandois, who, in August 1096, led his army from France to Bari, above the heel of Italy. From there he crossed the Adriatic and eventually, after a storm had wrecked several ships, reached the Byzantine port of Dyrrhachium. Hugh was greeted cordially by the local Byzantine governor and escorted east along the Via Egnatia, the old Roman road once travelled by St Paul, to Constantinople. There Emperor Alexius received him with friendship and generous gifts, although it is also suggested that Hugh was effectively put under house arrest. The unexpectedly early arrival of Hugh compelled the emperor to face up to the fact that his request for help from the west was resulting in large armies of men, already causing disturbances *en route* to Constantinople, and not the select bands of mercenaries he had been hoping for. How would he control these potentially dangerous westerners? His best ploy, he realized, was to persuade the crusader princes to swear a solemn oath that they would be his vassals and hand over to him any former Byzantine territories now under Turkish control. In return he would promise military support, food and guides. With Hugh, Alexius struck lucky: the French prince immediately agreed to the oath – his colleagues would be much more reluctant.

The next crusader princes to leave the west were Godfrey of Bouillon and his brother Baldwin, who arrived at Constantinople just before Christmas, 1096, and camped along the Golden Horn outside the city walls. At first Godfrey resisted taking the oath of allegiance, but after armed clashes between his men and the Byzantines he consented. Alexius then had the Franks ferried across the Bosphorus to keep them out of harm's way.

As more crusaders arrived, Alexius again manoeuvred their leaders into taking the oath before shipping them across to Asia. They included Bohemond and his band of Normans. With his imposing physique, spine-chilling laugh and ambiguous answers to questions, Bohemond gave Alexius the most cause for concern. From previous conflicts with the Normans, the Byzantine emperor knew they were warriors to be reckoned with, capable of ruthlessness and deviousness in equal measure; so he was relieved when Bohemond, eager to ingratiate himself with the emperor for his own benefit, took the oath. More formidable, though, in terms of numbers was the army of Raymond of Toulouse, who arrived on April 21, 1097, along with Adhémar, bishop of Le Puy, the pope's representative. Pressed by Alexius to take the oath, Raymond at first hesitated – after all, his initial crusading oath had been to Urban – but eventually agreed to swear a modified version of the oath. Finally, after the last crusader troops from northern France had been taken across the Bosphorus to join their fellow fighters, Alexius could reflect on a job well done. Thousands of

ABOVE *Godfrey of Bouillon, the duke of Lower Lorraine, was one of the principal leaders of the First Crusade. After the capture of Jerusalem in 1099, he ruled the city as "advocate of the Holy Sepulchre", but died after a year in office.*

OPPOSITE
Constantinople, now Istanbul, was the greatest city of the medieval world. This map shows the strength of its walls and the great domed church of Haghia Sophia in the east of the city.

Frankish soldiers had passed through his lands and capital city with minimal disturbance and their leaders had sworn their allegiance to him, although the pressure he applied could not but cause resentment in some cases. And whether they would honour their word was another matter.

THE GREAT PUSH

According to the chroniclers, the crusader army encamped in Asia ready for the great push toward Palestine consisted of something in the region of 100,000 fighting men and non-combatants (including priests and women), but modern historians believe it was less than half that number. Even so, it was a magnificent host, lacking little in equipment and nothing in motivation and courage. Only the lack of a universally respected supreme commander was a cause for concern – the bitter quarrels and jockeying for power that would surface consistently between rival leaders were to undermine the war effort.

In May 1097, the massed columns of the crusaders at last rolled south toward their first objective, the city of Nicaea, seat of the Seljuk sultan Kilij Arslan, whose suburbs had previously been ravaged by members of the People's Crusade. As chance would have it, the crusaders' arrival before the city's walls coincided with the absence of the sultan, who was away fighting other Turks. But Nicaea, with its massive walls and towers, proved a tough nut to crack, even after the Franks had successfully fought off Kilij Arslan's relief force (and had catapulted the severed heads of dead Turks into the city to sap the defenders' morale). In the end, it took a Byzantine blockade of the lake on the edge of which Nicaea stood, and which provided a supply route to the city, to make the defenders capitulate. Wisely, the latter insisted on surrendering to the emperor and not to the Franks, who, deprived of their eagerly anticipated orgy of destruction and pillaging, were reduced to muttering darkly about Byzantine treachery.

Nevertheless, a victory was a victory, and with buoyant spirits the crusaders set off on their trek south-eastward, travelling in two groups across the Anatolian plateau, a great barren, treeless wilderness, freezing in winter, torrid in summer. In the vanguard marched the Normans Bohemond and Tancred and others, while Godfrey of Bouillon, Raymond of Toulouse and the rest of the crusaders followed, a day's march behind.

By this time Kilij Arslan was under no illusion that these new foes were made of sterner stuff than the rabble he had encountered the year before. Rallying his forces, he attacked the camp of Bohemond and Tancred at dawn on July 1, 1097, near the small settlement of Dorylaeum, about 70 miles (112 km) south-east of Nicaea. With their fast, light, mobile cavalry and long-range bows, the Turks were always tricky opponents to counter. Courageous and hardy, they were also shrewd and quick to grasp that they would struggle to defeat the heavier and more powerful crusader knights in pitched battle. Their tactics often revolved around luring mounted knights into ambushes by feigned retreats or else isolating small groups of them so that they could be picked off more easily.

As the Turks bore down on Bohemond and his men, there was a real chance of a Christian catastrophe and the derailment of the whole crusade. Bohemond, however, quickly perceived the imminent danger and organized his men in an effective defensive formation. He also sent an urgent message to the other army group to come as soon as possible. While women supplied the parched, beleaguered knights with water, the Normans and their fellow fighters managed to hang on long enough for Godfrey, Raymond and Adhémar to take the Turks by surprise and rout them. From now on Kilij Arslan, realizing that it was folly to oppose the Franks in the open, resorted to a scorched-earth policy to hinder their advance.

THE ROAD TO ANTIOCH

This second resounding victory helped to offset the hardships that now took an increasing toll on the Franks. Relentless heat, thirst and hunger turned their march into a survival of the fittest. Donkeys, mules and oxen dropped dead, and men were reduced to eating their pack-horses for food and chewing thorn-bush branches in the hope of finding moisture. Then, in mid-August 1097, the city of Iconium (modern Konya), deserted by the Turks, loomed up like a shimmering oasis in the desert. The crusaders were not disappointed when they arrived there, finding plentiful orchards and streams, and a secure place where they could eat, drink and rest for a few days.

Back on the road, the Franks saw off a half-hearted Turkish attack at Heraclea, about 100 miles (160 km) east of Iconium, and then had to decide the best way of proceeding to Antioch in Syria, their first major military objective. Basically, there was a choice of two routes: the southern one was shorter but more steep and hazardous, going through the pass known as the Cilician Gates in the Taurus Mountains; the other was longer but less daunting and held out the prospect of a decent road from Caesarea in Cappadocia across the Anti-Taurus Mountains then south to Antioch. In the end, Baldwin, Godfrey's brother, and Tancred opted for the shorter route, while the rest settled for the longer one. After capturing various towns and quarrelling among themselves, Tancred and Baldwin went their separate ways, with Tancred rejoining the main army at Antioch and Baldwin becoming count of Edessa (see Box, p. 32).

BELOW *The bleak and barren Taurus mountains in the region of Cilicia in Anatolia were a demanding natural barrier for the crusaders on their eastward march to Syria.*

LEFT The Norman crusader Tancred, having split from the main army, captured the city of Tarsus in 1097. He is shown receiving the city's key in this 14th-century illumination.

While Tancred and Baldwin were busy creating and feathering their nests, the main crusader army had been making its way slowly and laboriously southward to Antioch. By October 1097 they reached the walls of what had been one of the great cities of the Roman Empire, the place where the word "Christian" was first coined. Protected by the River Orontes to the north and by a hillside, on which its citadel was built, to the south, and surrounded by imposing fortifications, Antioch was to be a major test of the crusaders' courage and endurance. Inside its walls the Turkish governor, Yaghi-Siyan, presided over a population of mainly Greek, Armenian and Syrian Christians, some of whom hated their co-religionists more than the Turks. He was well supplied with food from the fields and orchards that lay within the city perimeter and water, stored in giant reservoirs. Yet although his position was virtually unassailable, Yaghi-Siyan recognized the seriousness of the threat before him.

The crusaders might have made an immediate assault on the city if Raymond had had his way, but instead they opted for a long siege, which nearly ended in disaster. As winter approached, the Franks' morale dimmed and guttered. To feed their host, countless foraging parties had to be sent into the surrounding countryside and were vulnerable to lightning sorties by the Turkish defenders. By Christmas, rations were so low that it was decided that Bohemond and Robert of Flanders should take a sizeable number of troops to conduct a large-scale foraging expedition while Raymond and the rest of the army continued the siege. Learning that the Frankish army was split, the Turks sallied forth to make a surprise assault on the besiegers and were fought off only with great difficulty. Meanwhile Bohemond and Robert had problems of their own, encountering a substantial Turkish relief force. Incurring heavy losses, they managed to beat a retreat to Antioch, but with little to show for their efforts.

BALDWIN: COUNT OF EDESSA

Having split off from the main crusader army to indulge in some freelance fighting and pillaging, Baldwin of Boulogne had to hurry back to the main army at Marash to attend to his ominously sick wife and children. Despite their subsequent deaths, he decided to carry on with his ambition to gain a permanent foothold in Outremer and again took his leave of the main army. He headed east into country populated by Christian Armenians, who regarded the Frankish crusaders as glorious liberators from the Turkish yoke. Eventually, Baldwin was invited by Thoros, the Armenian prince of the city of Edessa, situated between the Tigris and Euphrates rivers, to be his co-ruler. After the crusader arrived in the city in February 1098, Thoros consolidated their agreement by adopting him as his son and heir.

It was not long before Baldwin's monopoly of power was complete. Hated by his people, Thoros was murdered in a popular uprising in March of the same year, and Baldwin – who may have been implicated in Thoros's death – was asked to take up the reins of government. He accepted and, as the new count of Edessa, became the first crusader to win a state in the east, if not quite the Holy Land itself.

Depressed, alarmed by an earthquake, and sodden to the skin after weeks of rain, the crusaders began to wonder whether they had incurred the displeasure of God – but the remedial fast that was imposed failed to improve morale. As people died from hunger, desertions occurred and, it was said, some turned to cannibalism. Even Bohemond threatened to leave, although this seems to have been a bargaining ploy to get the others to agree to his being lord of Antioch if and when it fell. Yet not all was gloom and doom. In February 1098 a Muslim relief force under the emir of the Syrian city of Aleppo was destroyed, and some food supplies arrived from Cyprus at Antioch's port of St Simeon. Then, on March 4, an English-led fleet arrived at St Simeon with more supplies and siege equipment, enabling the crusaders to tighten their stranglehold on the city. Even so, little progress was made, and in the end the city was to fall by treachery.

It so happened that Bohemond had made contact with an Armenian convert to Islam named Firouz, a member of Yagi-Siyan's entourage who bore a grudge against his master. Firouz agreed to deliver the city to the Franks. But it was a race against time, because the Turkish governor of Mosul, a man named Kerbogha, was reported to be advancing on Antioch with a large army. On June 2, 1098, Firouz was ready to carry out his betrayal. According to a carefully worked-out plan – which could have been taken from the pages of the *Iliad* – Bohemond set off eastward to give the Antiochenes the impression that he was going to fight the advancing Kerbogha. But under cover of night he doubled back to the city and waited with his men outside the walls by the Tower of the Two Sisters, the place designated by Firouz because it was under his command. All the crusaders needed was an open, unguarded window, and that is exactly what they found as a number of them scaled a ladder up to the tower. Before long the knights had managed to open two of the city's gates, allowing the bulk of the army to pour in. By the end of the day every Turk had been killed, except those who escaped to the citadel on the hillside.

UNDER SIEGE

Yet the Frankish triumph was short-lived. No sooner had they claimed Antioch for the cross than they in turn were besieged by Kerbogha. Their position was extremely precarious – no stockpiles of food could be found in the city, and there were too few men to guard the walls in their entirety. Furthermore, hopes that help might have been forthcoming from Emperor Alexius were dashed when the latter decided that a venture in aid of what reports had told him was a lost cause was not worth the risk. Matters looked grim for the crusaders, but salvation came in an extraordinary way. On June 10, 1098, a peasant named Peter Bartholomew revealed to Bishop Adhémar that he had received a series of visions from St Andrew in which it was revealed to him

LEFT *Antioch had a Christian presence from the earliest days of the church. This grotto, dedicated to St Peter, lies at the bottom of the hillside on which the city's citadel stood.*

that the holy lance which had pierced Christ's side during the crucifixion lay hidden in the ground inside Antioch's cathedral of St Peter. Adhémar was sceptical. But then a priest named Stephen, whom Adhémar was more inclined to believe, reported that he, too, had had a vision in which Christ declared that help would come to the crusaders in five days' time if they turned away from sin. As news of the visions spread, so did the general excitement of expectation.

On June 14, a party of crusaders went to the cathedral and started digging the ground below the floor, but found nothing. As hopes of unearthing the lance diminished, Peter Bartholomew himself leapt into the trench and having told everyone to pray he suddenly held aloft, to the astonishment of all, a pointed metal shaft. How Peter did this is not known. But news of the "discovery" of the "lance" did wonders for the army's morale.

Although further visions received by Peter served to weaken rather than strengthen his credibility, one of them, enjoining the crusaders to attack the Muslims in five days' time, struck a chord with the commanders. Bohemond in particular had come to the conclusion that the Franks would have to force the issue by assaulting Kerbogha, especially after peace talks instigated by the Franks had failed. In fact Kerbogha himself was having problems keeping his coalition of assorted emirs intact – internal squabbles were not the sole preserve of the Christians. So on June 28, weak in limb but strong in heart, the Frankish army, accompanied by priests, trooped out of Antioch to confront the armies of Mosul, Aleppo, Damascus and Homs. Battle was joined along the line and after Kerbogha's flanking movement was anticipated and checked by the crusaders, the latter gained the upper hand. Driven by desperation and inspired, apparently, by miracles – ghostly knights on white horses led by St George were reportedly seen on the hillside – the Franks pressed hard against the Turkish ranks. And when several emirs decided to withdraw to fight another day, the Turks' retreat turned into panic and a rout.

With Antioch securely in Christian hands, the thorny question was now who should take possession of

ABOVE *Crusaders flee from a burning wooden fortress in front of the walls of Antioch during their siege of the city. Placed under the command of Raymond IV, the fortress was intended to stop Muslim defenders using the bridge over the Orontes River.*

it? The crusaders' oaths required them to cede the city to Emperor Alexius, but Bohemond argued that since the emperor had not come to their aid he did not deserve it. Raymond, who resented Bohemond's own unsubtle push for personal power, disagreed. But most of the crusaders backed Bohemond, holding that, as the principal architect of their victory, it was he more than anyone else who deserved Antioch. Unfortunately, Bishop Adhémar, who was probably the only person with enough spiritual gravitas and sympathetic diplomacy to settle the issue, died in an epidemic.

As the months passed, the crusaders spent their time subduing neighbouring towns and castles but were still unable to decide the fate of Antioch – an invitation to the pope to come and sort out their differences proved fruitless. At a grand council in St Peter's Cathedral on November 5, Bohemond and Raymond were still at loggerheads, even though both felt pressure from the rank-and-file soldiers, who were exasperated by their bickering leaders and desperate to push on to

Jerusalem. The siege of the nearby town of Maarat, conducted in part to keep the soldiers occupied, ended in victory for the crusaders, but it was also an occasion for further wrangling and bitterness between Raymond's southern Frenchmen and Bohemond's Normans.

The in-fighting was only resolved in January 1099, when Raymond, having failed to get the other crusader leaders to serve under him, and resigned to leaving Bohemond behind in possession of Antioch, marched out of Maarat at the head of his troops, heading south for Jerusalem. The count of Toulouse walked barefoot, as befitted a pilgrim. Inspired, or shamed, by his example, most of the crusader commanders joined him. Only Baldwin, count of Edessa, and Bohemond, effectively prince of Antioch, stayed behind in their newly founded realms.

THE FALL OF JERUSALEM

Raymond's march to Jerusalem was relatively painless compared to the struggles faced in Anatolia and northern Syria. By and large the crusaders either captured the towns and castles that lay in their way or accepted treaties on favourable terms, receiving money, food and guides in return for peace. The exception was the town of Arqa, about 40 miles (65 km) east of the port of Tripoli. There the crusaders became bogged down in a fruitless siege which Raymond stubbornly refused to lift. There, too, the crusaders received a letter from Emperor Alexius informing them that he was planning to join the crusade in June. Raymond was in favour of waiting for him to arrive, but he was outnumbered by those who were eager to reach Jerusalem. In fact Alexius, more interested in Anatolia than Palestine, and disgusted by the way the crusaders had broken their oaths of allegiance at Antioch, was engaged in a diplomatic balancing act. While keeping in contact with the crusaders, he was also in communication with the Fatimids of Egypt, who at this time were in possession of Palestine. Fatimid delegates had also approached the Franks vis-à-vis a treaty, but had been rebuffed.

Finally abandoning the siege of Arqa, the crusaders continued south, making terms with, or bypassing, cities such as Sidon, Tyre and Acre. At Ramleh they branched eastward for Jerusalem, now only about 50 miles (80 km) away. On the morning of June 7, 1099, they reached the summit of a hill, traditionally called Monjoie, from which they could catch their first glimpse of the holy city, glimmering in the distance. A few hours later they were camped by the walls. The interval of time between Urban's speech at Clermont and the crusaders' arrival at Jerusalem was just over three and a half years; and by this time the once-mighty force was down to an estimated 15,000 men.

Yet there was still a formidable hurdle to negotiate. The Fatimid governor of Jerusalem, Iftikhar ad-Dawla, was in a strong position. The city's walls had recently been reinforced. Large quantities of food and water had been stored up, and sheep, goats and cattle from the surrounding villages had been driven into the city to provide extra provisions and to deprive the enemy of fresh meat. The crusaders also found that the local wells had been poisoned. And Iftikhar had sent a message to Egypt urgently requesting military aid.

After the failure of an initial fierce but unsustained assault, the crusaders set about laying siege to the city, soon greatly heartened by the arrival of Genoese and English ships at the port of Jaffa, about 40 miles (65 km) to the west, with much-needed munitions and equipment. The key to the crusaders' plan of assault was the construction of three siege engines – large, wooden mobile towers clad in fire-retardant oxhides and equipped with drawbridges that could be dropped down on top of the city's walls, allowing specially picked troops to race across and establish a bridgehead. By early July preparations for an all-out assault intensified as news arrived that a large Muslim relief force was heading north from Egypt. At the same time, as hunger, disease and the heat took their toll, the crusaders' spirits sank. Then, when their morale had reached rock bottom, a priest named Peter Desiderius reported having a vision in which the late Bishop Adhémar ordered the crusaders to fast for a day then process barefoot and bare-headed around Jerusalem. If they did this in a spirit of repentance the city would fall to them in nine days.

On July 8, in obedience to this vision, the entire Christian army marched around the walls – in a manner reminiscent of the Israelites under Joshua at Jericho – while the Muslims hurled abuse and dung at them or spat on hastily made crosses or carried them on their backs in theatrical mockery. The act of penance seemed to inject a new determination into the Christians. With renewed vigour they set about finishing their siege towers and by the evening of July 14 the tower commanded by Raymond had been pushed up to a section of the southern wall, although the defenders repelled the attack.

The next morning, the crusaders resumed their assault, while rocks, incendiary arrows and "Greek fire" – a deadly cocktail of sulphur and resins often described as "medieval napalm" – rained down on them. After fierce fighting, the battle turned the crusaders' way when the Muslim defenders on the northern wall opposite the siege tower commanded by Godfrey of Bouillon were suddenly driven back by a fire. Seizing the opportunity, Godfrey ordered the tower's drawbridge to be lowered. Within minutes a squad of crusaders had crossed over to the walls and established a secure position, enabling more troops to swarm up from below on scaling ladders. Soon the crack in the defences became a gaping hole. The Christians inside the city opened up Herod's Gate and the rest of their comrades stormed in.

The rout turned into a massacre. Months of deprivation and stifled anticipation now turned the crusaders into packs of wolves, baying for blood. For the rest of the day and through the night no quarter was given. Women and children were cut down as if they were fighting men. The resident Jews, who had gathered in their synagogue for safety, were burnt alive. The sacred Dome of the Rock, with its golden cupola and the nearby mosque of al-Aqsa became abattoirs of mangled bodies. The only people who escaped the massacre were the Muslim governor and his entourage, who had managed to bribe Raymond with large amounts of money to let them make their escape.

With their enemies annihilated and their aggression temporarily spent, the crusaders processed through the blood-wet streets to the Church of the Holy Sepulchre to fulfil their crusading vows and to give thanks to God for victory. Jerusalem had been returned to Christian hands. But the sublime victory had been marred by their subhuman savagery, encapsulated by the crusader Raymond d'Aguilers, who later wrote: "For those present, what was worse than the headless corpses and hacked-off limbs scattered all around was the sight of the victors themselves, soaked in blood, inspiring fear in all who met them."

ABOVE Godfrey of Bouillon commands a wheeled siege tower in this medieval illumination. It was by means of Godfrey's tower that the crusaders gained a foothold on the walls of Jerusalem, leading to their victory.

A CRUSADER BASE

After their capture of Jerusalem the crusaders' leaders then had to decide quickly who should govern their conquest, especially since a Muslim counterattack was considered inevitable. The two most suitable candidates were Raymond and Godfrey, and it was the latter who was eventually chosen, much to the chagrin of his rival. The other key post was that of patriarch, the spiritual leader of the city, and the choice fell on Arnulf of Rohes. He proceeded to fill all available ecclesiastical posts with Latin clerics, to the detriment of the Greek Orthodox clergy (he also offended members of minority heretical Christian churches, such as the Jacobites, Copts and Armenians).

Godfrey's immediate concern was manpower – a problem that would beset the Frankish states in Outremer, or the Latin east, for the duration of their history. Although, a few weeks after the capture of Jerusalem, the army was strong enough to defeat a Fatimid army near Ascalon on the coast, many crusaders began to leave the Holy Land to go home, having fulfilled their vows. Those who remained included Baldwin of Edessa, Bohemond of Antioch, Tancred, who was given lands in Galilee, and Raymond. Godfrey himself ruled Jerusalem for only a year before becoming ill and dying on July 18, 1100. His place was taken by his brother, Baldwin of Edessa, who, with far fewer scruples than his brother about being appointed the sovereign of the city of which Christ was considered to be the true monarch, was duly crowned king of Jerusalem on Christmas day, 1100.

3

AT THE GATES OF DAMASCUS

From the western point of view, the First Crusade had reached a glorious, if bloody, climax with the capture of Jerusalem in July 1099. After some 400 years of Islamic rule the city was now back under Christian control. Muslims and Jews were banned from living in the city, and mosques and synagogues metamorphosed into churches. When the news of the victory filtered back to western Europe there was general rejoicing, although Pope Urban II, the prime mover behind the crusade, died before he heard of the victory.

In the euphoric aftermath of the triumph, a new wave of crusaders, from Lombardy in northern Italy, France and elsewhere, set out from September 1100 onwards to experience some of the action and, they hoped, the spoils that their Christian brothers had enjoyed. This latest war effort, however, succeeded only in diminishing the achievements of the First Crusade. In the terrible heat and wildernesses of Anatolia, a combination of poor leadership, exhaustion, hunger and fierce attacks by the Turks left these latest crusaders dead, captured or floundering for safety. Instead of establishing a land route from Constantinople to Syria, they ensured that until the Second Crusade in the late 1140s crusaders would have no choice but to travel by ship to the Holy Land.

CONSOLIDATING THE KINGDOMS

Meanwhile, in the Latin kingdom of Jerusalem, King Baldwin I had to set about strengthening his realm and the precarious position of the Franks in the east. Apart from Baldwin's kingdom, crusader settlements comprised the counties of Edessa and Tripoli and the principality of Antioch. Edessa, lying about 50 miles (80 km) east of the Euphrates, was mostly populated by Christian Armenians, but it was dangerously out on a limb and susceptible to Muslim attacks. About 150 miles (240 km) south-west of Edessa lay Antioch, governed by Bohemond, although after the latter's capture and temporary imprisonment by the Turks his nephew Tancred was made the city's regent. Antioch's political and social elite were Norman Italians, who ruled over native Armenian and Syrian Christians and Muslims. South of the city on the coast lay the county of Tripoli, which had been founded by Raymond of Toulouse and whose southern extent almost reached Beirut, which lay in Baldwin's realm. His kingdom of Jerusalem included Galilee, the Dead Sea region and a series of castles that extended to the Red Sea.

Baldwin's principal concern was a lack of manpower and the inescapable fact that the crusader states basically formed a long narrow island hemmed in by the Mediterranean to the west and a sea of Islam to the east. Yet for about 20 years or more after the fall of Jerusalem the various Muslim powers, through their chronic lack of unity, gave the Franks an extended breathing space and a chance to consolidate and organize themselves. Crucially, there was a profound cultural and ideological divide as well as a bitter rivalry between the Abbasid caliphate in Baghdad, which was a bastion of orthodox Sunni Islam, and the Fatimid caliphate in Egypt, which was Shiite. There

RIGHT *King Baldwin I and his knights join battle with their Muslim foes in this illustration from the 15th-century* Chronicles of the Emperors *by David Aubert.*

40

were also numerous rivalries between smaller regional Muslim states, and the Franks' ability to play one off against the other was a key strategy for survival. In Syria, towns such as Aleppo, Mosul and Damascus, with their unloved Seljuk Turkish governors, technically acknowledged the authority of the Abbasid caliph (who was in fact in thrall to the Seljuk Turkish sultan). But the caliph was often powerless to stop, or indifferent to, wars between the states, as local emirs tried to expand or preserve their power.

Benefiting from Muslim disunity, the Franks realized that to guarantee the vital influx of new settlers, pilgrims and material resources, the ports of the Syrian and Palestinian seaboards – a 600-mile (965-km) stretch of coastline – would have to be secured. As it stood, only Antioch's port of St Simeon and Jaffa were in Christian hands. The problem was that most of the ports had formidable fortifications and, most importantly, they could easily be resupplied by Muslim navies from Egypt as well as neighbouring towns. The crusaders, who were basically landlubbers with little naval experience, knew that unless the ports were blockaded by sea their siege attempts were doomed to fail. The problem was eventually solved by the dynamic Italian maritime republics of Genoa, Pisa and Venice, which, motivated by religious piety and the reward of substantial tax and trading concessions, were able to mount effective blockades. Caesarea, Acre, Sidon and almost all the other Muslim ports fell into Christian hands during the first decade of Outremer's history. Only Tyre and Ascalon held out until 1123 and 1153 respectively.

THE GOVERNMENT OF THE LATIN EAST

With the ports secure, allowing the influx of people and supplies from Europe, and with their internal borders relatively well demarcated by rivers, mountains or imposing hilltop castles, the crusaders were able to focus more easily on developing a way of life in their new environment. It is true that they always had to live with an ever-present threat of war and violence, variously arising from expansionist dreams, changing alliances, the sudden transfers of power after the death of a ruler, and dynastic squabbling, all of which were endemic in both Christian and Muslim spheres. Yet as the years went by, the Franks began to evolve a *modus vivendi* that combined ingrained western ideas and habits with grafted-on oriental customs.

The basic political and social system adopted by the Franks, which later historians have termed "feudal", was already common in western Europe. Feudalism was based on a hierarchical web of personal relationships, established by oath, and carrying rights and obligations on both sides. In simplest terms it meant that in return for a grant of land, or fief, a knight or other noble would be obliged to give military service – crucial in the Latin east – and other assistance to his social superior. At the top of the feudal pyramid stood the king, and below him came princes, dukes and other senior nobles, then the lesser nobility, the knights, and at the bottom, the peasants, who in return for protection were obliged to work their lords' land. In the Latin east, kings of Jerusalem were technically overlords of both Edessa and Tripoli. Antioch was supposed to have been a vassal state of the Byzantine emperor, but it kept asserting its independence. It also had to remain on good terms with the kingdom of Jerusalem, to whom it would turn most often for military help. In general, the volatile politics of the area made loyalties fluid and often ephemeral.

The government of the Latin kingdom was centred on the High Court, where the king would meet with his noble vassals to discuss the affairs of state. The court dispensed justice and debated

HOSPITALLERS AND TEMPLARS

From a Christian point of view, one of the most important occurrences during the period between the First and Second Crusades was the founding of the military orders: the Knights of St John (Hospitallers), distinguished by their black mantles and eight-pointed crosses; and the Knights of the Temple (Templars), who wore white mantles emblazoned with red crosses. Combining the western Christian ideals of chivalry and monasticism, the orders (later joined by the Teutonic Knights) evolved to become the most potent fighting force in the Latin east. Originally concentrating on the care and protection of pilgrims, the Hospitallers and Templars grew to become virtually standing armies – the only ones in the Latin east – renowned for their discipline and courage. However, their relative independence meant that they often pursued policies that were self-serving rather than designed for the greater good of the Latin kingdom as a whole.

The Knights Hospitaller developed from a hostel founded in Jerusalem in 1070 by pious merchants of the Italian town of Amalfi. Run mainly by Amalfi citizens and headed by a master, the hostel offered hospitality and medical care to the poor. After the fall of Jerusalem to the Christians in 1099, the current master of the hostel, a man named Gerard, transformed the institution into an order dedicated to St John the Baptist, which was formally recognized by the pope in 1113. The charitable concerns of the Hospitallers were to remain a constant throughout its history. But by 1130 the order had also become a military organization, dedicated to protecting pilgrims and, later, fighting the Muslims whenever necessary. Recruits had to swear monastic vows of poverty, chastity and obedience as well as an oath to fight the infidel. Over time the order's finances were built up by gifts from pilgrims and wealthy donors back in Europe as well as by grants of land from Outremer nobles. The knights went on to acquire and fortify great castles such as Krak des Chevaliers, Belvoir and al-Marqab.

After the fall of Acre in 1291, the Knights of St John moved to Cyprus before establishing themselves on the island of Rhodes. From there they continued to fight against the Muslims until, after an epic siege in 1522, they were compelled to leave by the Ottoman sultan Suleyman the Magnificent. In 1530 Malta then became their principal headquarters, remaining so until Napoleonic times.

Associates and rivals of the Hospitallers, the Knights of the Temple were established in about 1120 by a group of French knights led by Hugh of Payns specifically to protect pilgrims travelling along the Jaffa to Jerusalem road. King Baldwin II allotted them quarters in what was called the Temple of Solomon (actually the al-Aqsa mosque on Temple Mount) in Jerusalem, from which they derived their name. Like the Hospitallers, they also took vows of poverty, chastity and obedience.

What boosted the Templars' reputation in their early years was the support of Bernard of Clairvaux, who helped to draw up their monastic rule (approved in 1128) and also lauded them in his pamphlet, *On the Praise of the New Knighthood*. In this he contrasts the ideal of the Templar against the reality of the worldly knight, with his love of fashion, pomp and fripperies. By contrast, Bernard claims, the Templar lives a stern, sober life, rejecting games such as chess and dice and pastimes such as story-telling, and refraining from laughter, whispering and "suppressed giggling". After Bernard's paean of praise, a flood of recruits joined the order, which comprised three classes: noble-born knights; sergeants, who were fighting men of non-noble stock; and chaplains.

Formally constituted in 1129 and answerable only to the pope, the Templars grew into a rich, powerful and therefore often resented organization, headed by a grand master, with their military operations extending into Europe. After the fall of Acre in 1291, with their *raison d'être* undermined, they became the target of King Philip IV of France, who appears to have coveted their lands and wealth. Philip accused them of heresy, seemingly on the basis of unfounded rumours, and pressured the reluctant Pope Clement V into dissolving the order in 1312. Two years later the Templars' grand master Jacques de Molay and a number of his associates were burned as relapsed heretics in Paris.

ABOVE *Mounted Knights Templar, with crosses on their mantles, ride determinedly from their stronghold to confront the enemy in this 12th-century French fresco.*

matters such as foreign policy and raising armies. There were also *parlements*, composed of leading barons, churchmen and others, which occasionally met to formulate policy on matters such as taxation and diplomacy.

Despite incessant infighting, the Franks usually pulled together when they were sure they faced a serious Muslim threat, tacitly acknowledging that there were too few of them to stand alone. Scholars have estimated that there were probably no more than 700 knights obliged to give military service in the kingdom of Jerusalem at any given time, with about 1,400 for Antioch, Edessa and Tripoli put together. While a total of 2,000 knights may seem a small number it must be remembered that with their heavy armour, array of weapons – including lance, sword and mace – and powerful horses, knights were the tanks of the medieval world. Also, the Frankish armies were constantly being bulked up on a seasonal basis by new arrivals from Europe. There were, in addition, the armies of the military orders, the Knights Templar and Knights Hospitaller (see Box), who added greatly to the available military strength, if not manpower. To them must be added mercenaries, armed pilgrims from Europe, and the navies of the Italian maritime communities of Venice, Genoa and Pisa.

BELOW *The Church of the Holy Sepulchre in Jerusalem, which covered the sites of Jesus' death and resurrection, was the most sacred spot in Christendom. The crusaders literally left their mark on it - carving crosses and other graffiti on its walls.*

THE FIRST SETTLERS

Most of the Frankish population of the Latin east, which has been estimated at a maximum of 140,000, lived in towns and cities, where they might work as merchants, tailors, bakers, shoemakers, carpenters, shopkeepers or masons. Indeed, the Franks were impressive builders, and churches such as the reconstructed Holy Sepulchre in Jerusalem and the Cathedral of Tortosa or Tartus in the county of Tripoli, and castles such as the Hospitaller stronghold of Krak des Chevaliers, still bear witness to their flair for stately and pragmatic architecture.

Within the Christian towns the Frankish nobility remained aloof from the ordinary townsfolk – the Greeks, Arabs, Turks, Armenians and Egyptians who belonged to one of the three great monotheistic religions: Islam, Christianity (in its various orthodox and schismatic hues) and Judaism. Although when it came to conjugal relations Frankish nobles stayed within their own circles, there was a degree of intermarrying between indigenous Christian families and the lower social echelons of the Franks, especially in Edessa, where Armenian Christians formed most of the population.

In the first 20 years after the capture of Jerusalem, the Latin Church established itself in Outremer and managed to build or reconstruct ecclesiastical buildings with the help of Catholic churchmen and funds from Europe. Apart from encountering members of the Greek Orthodox Church, the Franks came across a number of different Christian sects, including Armenians, Syrian Jacobites, and a few Egyptian Copts, who were monophysites – that is they believed that Christ had one, single divine nature, against the orthodox teaching that he had a double (divine and human) nature. At first the Latin Church was tolerant of its Orthodox co-religionists, but this changed, especially when aggression by the Byzantines toward the Franks made Orthodox churchmen suspect in crusader-held settlements. There were never many practising Catholics in Palestine, despite some conversions by members of other churches – probably seen as a means of surmounting the otherwise inferior legal status they suffered. There was also a disproportion of higher clergy to ordinary priests: in the words of historian Jonathan Riley-Smith, "The Latin Church ... like a banana republic, had far too many generals for the troops available."

Living alongside the Franks and the ordinary townsfolk, and keeping very much to themselves, were the communes of the Italian republics. The merchants, middlemen, sailors and priests of Genoa, Pisa and Venice, as a reward for their cities' contribution toward the war effort, were allotted streets or whole quarters in many towns. They were also given certain privileges, such as exemption from local taxes and customs duties and the right to administer their own affairs. The Frankish cities were certainly no substitutes for the great emporia of Alexandria and Constantinople, but nevertheless the Italians did well out of the spices (in particular), perfumes, incense, dye-stuffs, textiles and other goods that flowed into their storehouses from caravans from Damascus and elsewhere, ready to be shipped off to Europe.

A smaller percentage of the Franks – but still a significant one, as recent research has shown – lived in the country where, it seems from a report by the twelfth-century Muslim traveller Ibn Jubayr, they made a positive impact. Passing through the region around Tyre, Ibn Jubayr reported seeing a series of villages and farms, with well-cultivated fields, owned by Muslims who were prospering under the Franks. He remarked that the Muslims paid less tax than they did before the Franks took over and also enjoyed a better system of justice than their brethren in Muslim-held territory. He also harboured the fear that these pleasant conditions might even result in Muslims transferring their political and religious allegiances – "May God preserve us from temptation!" he exclaims.

EAST MEETS WEST

Although the Franks were forbidden to marry Muslims (the punishment of castration was one of the deterrents) they inevitably absorbed many oriental habits and customs, especially those that were suited to the climate. Frankish nobles soon discovered the wisdom of protecting their armour from the burning sun by overlaying it with linen surcoats, as well as the practicality of putting on a cool silk burnous after returning home from campaign. Frankish women typically wore the oriental-style short, embroidered tunic, worn over a long undergarment. Both men and women kept warm in the surprisingly chilly winters with furs.

Frankish attitudes to hygiene changed radically in the Latin east. Back in Europe washing was not considered a priority, indeed it was often despised as a mark of effeminacy. But the crusaders soon began to discover the therapeutic pleasures of the public bath – similar to a modern Turkish bath – that was a normal part of Muslim life. To many European newcomers, the sight of settled crusaders using soap and gossiping in the bath halls, wearing silk and feasting on a diet of quinces, dates, figs, peaches, plums, almonds and other exotic foods was a shock to the system. James of Vitry, who became the bishop of Acre in the early thirteenth century, was probably not untypical when he declared that the local Christian aristocracy had been "brought up in luxury, soft and

AT THE GATES OF DAMASCUS

لو ترجنبه هذا الغلام الىك بان اخفف ثمنه عليك فان ماثى دهوان شي
واشترى ماجنت فنقلته المبلغ فقلته في اجارك كما انقدن الرخص الغال ولم

effeminate, more used to baths than battles, addicted to unclean and riotous living, clad like women in soft robes."

As well as Muslim dress, diet and hygiene, the Franks were also impressed by Muslim physicians. From the eighth century onwards the Muslims had initiated new techniques and approaches to medicine. The physician Razi (865–925), for example, was a pioneer in the treatment of smallpox and in his emphasis on the importance of diet and a clean environment. It is said that he recommended the site of a Baghdad hospital on the basis of hanging up pieces of raw meat in various places around the city then choosing the spot where the meat had putrefied most slowly. Muslim doctors were also ahead of their European counterparts in surgery, anaesthetics, drugs and ointments, which they made from plants and minerals. It is no wonder that the chronicler William of Tyre wrote that the Franks rejected the methods and medicines of their own doctors and trusted only "the Jews, Samaritans, Syrians and Saracens".

Physicians played a major role in the Latin east, where warfare, whether in the form of full-scale battles, minor skirmishes, raids, ambushes or single assassinations, was endemic. Even when they were not fighting, knights maintained their martial skills by going on hunts, engaging in falconry or holding tournaments. Armed and mounted, hunters would seek out lions, leopards and bears – still existing in Palestine at this time – as well as animals familiar from Europe, such as deer and wild boar. Tournaments, which combined the colour of the carnival with the military training of the assault course, were held in open spaces just outside the towns and consisted of jousting between individuals or between groups of knights. Occasionally there might be a *divertissement*: a Muslim chronicler named Usamah Ibn Munqidh reported seeing an occasion when two decrepit old women were made to run a race, with groups of knights goading them both on as they stumbled toward the finishing line and the prize – a scalded pig.

Usamah himself, a sensitive and observant traveller, made friends among the Franks – a testimony to the fact that Christians and Muslims, as they made increasing contact with each other, were sometimes able to appreciate their common humanity rather than emphasize their religious

and racial differences. Once when Usamah was visiting Christian-held Jerusalem he went to pray at the al-Aqsa mosque on Temple Mount. However, as he began to pray in the direction of Mecca, a Frank grabbed him and turned him roughly toward the east, saying "This is how we pray!" Fortunately for Usamah, some Knights Templar who were friends of his dragged the over-zealous Frank away, explaining that his bad manners were due to the fact that he had just arrived from Europe.

The incident neatly illustrates the pragmatic tolerance which the Outremer Franks often embraced, or were forced to embrace, through associating with the Muslims. Indeed, Frankish and Muslim nobles admired each other's fighting prowess and were known to hunt together. But encounters through common interests or pursuits or through trade led to little exchange of culture or scholarship between Christians and Muslims. The Arabic learning that did filter through to the west came not from Outremer but by way of Sicily, Moorish Spain and Constantinople.

Yet contact did help to breed tolerance, and this was in stark contrast to the bigotry frequently manifested by new arrivals from Europe, many of whom, full of religious zeal, were determined to attack and kill Muslims even if the political situation demanded calm and tactful diplomacy. Newcomers did not often fully appreciate the subtle process of orientalization undergone by their Frankish brothers, famously summed up by the chronicler Fulcher of Chartres (1058–1127): "We who had been westerners have become orientals – those who were Romans or Franks have become Galileans or Palestinians; and those who lived in Rheims or Chartres have now become citizens of Tyre or Acre. Already we have forgotten where we were born ... those who were once strangers here are now natives."

THE FIELD OF BLOOD

For a couple of decades the Franks profited from Muslim disunity. But after the death of Baldwin I in 1118 and the crowning of the count of Edessa – the late king's cousin and namesake – as King Baldwin II of Jerusalem, there came the first signs that Muslim apathy and fatalism in the face of the Frankish conquests were coming to an end. Something of a watershed encounter between the settlers and Muslims occurred in 1119 at the battle of the Field of Blood.

The conflict came about after Roger, the current Norman prince of Antioch (he was the nephew of Tancred), began exerting pressure on the strategic Muslim city of Aleppo, lying about 70 miles (112 km) to the east of Roger's capital. The Aleppans entrusted the defence of their city to a Turkish prince named Ilghazi, who formed an alliance with the city of Damascus. When Ilghazi then went on the offensive, mounting a raid on Antioch, Roger had two options: waiting for the reinforcements that had been sent by Baldwin at his urgent request; or leading his men out straightaway against the combined Muslim forces, which numbered some 40,000 men, about ten times the size of his own army.

Despite the urgings of the patriarch of Antioch to wait, Roger decided to go on the attack at once. Advancing toward the enemy, Roger set up camp for the night in open country; but, next morning, he found himself completely surrounded by Ilghazi's host. A break-out was the Franks' only chance of survival, but a desperate massed charge resulted in the escape of only a few knights, who took the news of the imminent slaughter back to Antioch. Almost the entire Antiochene army

ABOVE *Aleppo was one of the most important Muslim cities of Syria. The surviving narrow streets give an idea of what the medieval city must have looked like.*

ABOVE *Baldwin II was crowned king of Jerusalem in 1118. Here he is shown on a bronze Edessan coin wearing chain mail and a conical helmet.*

was killed on the spot, including Roger himself, or tortured to death later in the streets of Aleppo. In fact the disaster could have been much worse for the Franks if Ilghazi had marched at once on undefended Antioch. At it turned out, his delay allowed Baldwin enough time to reach the city and re-fortify it. Nevertheless, the defeat was a profound blow for the crusaders. The Muslims of Syria had conclusively destroyed the aura of the Franks' invincibility, showing that by cooperation they could more than match the Christians in pitched battle.

Although, with hindsight, the Field of Blood may be seen as a turning point, the crusaders did not know that at the time, and indeed within a few years they scored a singular triumph when they captured the powerful coastal city of Tyre in 1124. The Franks could not have accomplished this without a naval blockade, which was supplied by the Venetians, who stole a march on their rivals, the Genoese and Pisans, who were then at war with each other. After a four-month siege, during which the defenders were worn down by a lack of food and water, the city capitulated. In return for their efforts the Venetians received a third of Tyre, a payment of 300 gold bezants a year, exemption from customs duties and taxes (except one on pilgrims), and the right to trade freely.

THE REVIVAL OF *JIHAD*

If the Franks felt that the taking of Tyre had restored their military authority and the stability of the Latin east, they were much mistaken. For the 1120s saw the rise to power in Syria of Imad al-Din Zangi (or Zengi), who eventually came to govern both the cities of Mosul and Aleppo. An austere, astute man and a charismatic general, Zangi managed to utilize the growing sense of frustration felt by ordinary Muslims – especially the fugitives from cities newly captured by the Franks – with the inability of their leaders to counteract the westerners. This discontent was voiced in the mosques, and it seemed to some later Muslim writers that it was at this time that the idea of the "*jihad*" – literally "struggle" [to advance Islam] – or holy war against the Franks, which had been dormant in Muslim lands for centuries, was being re-awakened. This gave Zangi the spiritual and moral support he needed to wage a campaign against the Franks, a struggle that he conducted with discipline and tactical cunning. His soldiers were so well trained that it is said they marched as if between two invisible ropes. A network of spies in the major cities of foe and friend alike kept him informed of all relevant goings on. Even so, it should be noted that Zangi also spent a great deal of time and effort fighting Muslim rivals, which included his failed attempts to take the city of Damascus.

The rise of Zangi coincided with an uncertain period for the crusaders. In 1131 Baldwin II died and was replaced by a lesser man, Fulk V of Anjou, who had married Baldwin's daughter, Melisende. Fulk quickly had to deal with internal squabbles within the kingdom, but these problems soon paled in comparison with the threat from Zangi. In 1137 Fulk found himself besieged by Zangi in the castle of Montferrand, north-east of Tripoli, a result of Fulk's attempt to come to the assistance of the count of Tripoli, Raymond II. Although there was a Christian relief force on its way, Fulk did not know this and, with food running out, he asked Zangi for terms, fearing the worst. To his amazement, Zangi asked only for the castle – in return the king and his soldiers could go free. In fact Zangi had made a shrewder bargain than it seemed, for without loss of life he had gained a strategically important stronghold.

THE BYZANTINE BACKLASH

The same year, 1137, saw the stirring of the Byzantine emperor John II, who was intent on restoring imperial fortunes in Anatolia, where he fought the Danishmend Turks. He was also eager to remind the crusaders that former Byzantine territories (such as Antioch) were rightfully, by oaths they had sworn, his vassal states. In August 1137 he arrived at the gates of Antioch and invested the city with his huge army; it was not long before the city's ruler Raymond (of Poitiers), advised by King Fulk, gritted his teeth and paid the emperor homage. Satisfied with this response, John and his troops retreated westward to Cilicia in Anatolia for the winter before returning to Syria the following year, this time to confront Zangi. To do so effectively, John needed the committed support of Raymond of Antioch and Joscelin II, count of Edessa. But not only did these rival Frankish magnates loathe each other and fear that the other might gain a special relationship with the emperor, both men dreaded the prospect of the emperor increasing his power at their expense.

With only half-hearted assistance from the Franks, John had to confront Zangi with effectively one arm tied behind his back, and his campaign duly stalled while he was besieging the town of Shaizar. Although the uncooperative Raymond and Joscelin were present, they sulkily played dice away from the action, forcing the furious and frustrated emperor to raise the siege and decline risking a battle with Zangi and his relief force. John eventually withdrew from Syria, only to return in 1142, this time to teach Raymond a lesson for his recalcitrance and duplicity. Yet after his arrival, John found there was not enough campaigning time before the winter season, so he retreated back to Cilicia. There, while preparing to advance again in the spring of 1143, he died in a hunting accident. Bizarrely, a few months later, Fulk, King of Jerusalem, also died while out hunting. His widow, Queen Melisende, took sole responsibility for government until her and Fulk's 13-year-old son was crowned Baldwin III at Christmas 1143.

With the two most powerful and influential Christian rulers in the east dead, Zangi was not long in hammering home his advantage. He invaded the county of Edessa the following autumn and besieged the city itself while Count Joscelin happened to be away. After a four-week siege Edessa, the first crusader state to be established, became the first to fall back into the hands of the Muslims at Christmas 1144. Zangi became a Muslim hero; but he enjoyed his new-found status for only a year and a half before being murdered by a vengeful court eunuch. The respite the crusaders might have hoped for after the death of such a brilliant and ruthless opponent did not materialize. Zangi's son, Nur al-Din, was a chip off the old block, one who would inspire the Franks with even greater dread than his father had done.

THE SECOND CRUSADE

News of the fall of Edessa was greeted with shock and dismay in the west. Eventually, in response, Pope Eugenius issued a crusade encyclical in December 1145, specifically addressed to King Louis VII of France, calling for a new expedition to help the Christians in the east. At first the reaction to this new clarion call was weak, and it took the high

ST BERNARD OF CLAIRVAUX

The person who did more than anyone else to stir the hearts of the French and German nobility to undertake the Second Crusade, Bernard of Clairvaux was the most influential churchman of the twelfth century. A Cistercian monk and theologian with a penchant for mysticism, Bernard was charismatic, energetic and blessed with a golden tongue with which he charmed and chastized in equal measure Europe's kings, popes and nobles. His fascination was such that it is said that "mothers hid their sons, wives their husbands, companions their friends" to stop them being led away by his persuasive rhetoric.

Born in 1090 of a well-to-do Burgundian family, Bernard became a Cistercian monk at the abbey of Cîteaux (Latin Cistercium) near Dijon. At the age of 25 he left to found, nearby, the Cistercian house of Clairvaux, with which he became associated for the rest of his life. There he maintained a strict regime that attracted many new disciples, eager for the rigour the Cistercians were bringing to monastic life. For by the eleventh century, many monasteries had become too worldly and, in reaction, new orders such as the Augustinian canons sought to return to a more primitive style, with more stress on poverty and discipline. The Cistercians, or White Monks, were probably the most successful of the reformers. They built their monasteries in remote parts of the countryside and emphasized the importance of manual labour, strict diet and silence. Through good leadership and organization, the order expanded rapidly: more than 500 houses were established by the end of the twelfth century.

Never shy of entering ecclesiastical and political controversies, Bernard backed Innocent II in his struggle with Anacletus II for the throne of St Peter, rallying support for him from most of the major European powers. Then in 1140 he was entrusted with the prosecution of the famous controversial theologian Peter Abelard, who had been accused of heretical teachings. The showdown between the two men took place at a church council at Sens; but the potentially explosive drama was deflated by Abelard's decision not to defend himself – he retired from the council, which then formally condemned him.

In 1146 Bernard again used his passionate eloquence, this time to preach the Second Crusade, persuading Louis VII and Conrad III and their nobles to launch an enormous expedition to the east. However, after the failure of the crusade, Bernard's reputation suffered. During his last years his mood was deeply affected by the death of a number of friends, especially that of Pope Eugenius III, who had been a pupil of his. He himself died on August 20, 1153, at the age of 63.

BELOW *St Bernard of Clairvaux, the greatest churchman of his age, receives a vision of the Virgin Mary while he is writing a homily in this 15th-century Italian painting.*

reputation and forceful preaching of the Cistercian monk Bernard of Clairvaux, the greatest churchman of his time (see Box), to stir up the passions and mobilize a new Christian host. On March 31, 1146, Bernard preached to a huge crowd, which included King Louis and his nobles, in a field outside the French town of Vézelay. He read out Eugenius's encyclical, promised a full remission of sins and urged those present to join the crusade. Soon there were people crying out for crosses to sew onto their clothes. King Louis was the first to take the cross, quickly followed by his nobles, who up to this point had been dragging their feet over the whole enterprise. Then, as the enthusiastic demand outstripped the supply of material which had been brought along to make the crosses, Bernard dramatically had his own habit cut up into cruciform strips.

From Vézelay, Bernard proceeded to northern France and Flanders, preaching the crusade. He then moved to Germany to quell a bout of crusade-inspired anti-semitic violence. While he was there he decided to preach to the Germans and in particular Conrad III of Hohenstaufen, their king. At first Conrad, who had troubles of his own at home, especially from the house of Welf, held out against the force of Bernard's rhetoric. But at Christmas 1146 in Speyer, Bernard preached at Mass before the king, this time decisively. In a passionate crescendo, he turned toward Conrad and, as if taking the part of Christ himself, he asked: "Man, what more could I have done unto thee that I have not done?" Conrad melted before the heat of these words and promised to lead a German crusade.

The German king and his army left in May 1147 and headed east toward Constantinople, travelling across Hungary. Their progress was relatively trouble-free until the troops reached Byzantine territory, where their pillaging and marauding led to violence – much to the alarm of the Byzantine emperor Manuel I Comnenus. Conrad's unruly force, which included not only Germans but French-speaking Lorrainers and Slavs, eventually reached the Byzantine capital in September.

A month after Conrad's departure, Louis and his queen, the young, pretty, and dynamic Eleanor of Aquitaine (the future wife of Henry II of England and mother of Richard the Lionheart) set out with the French army and marched via

PREVIOUS PAGE *Melisende, the daughter of King Baldwin II of Jerusalem, marries the French noble Fulk V of Anjou in this illustration from the chronicler William of Tyre's* History of the Conquest of Jerusalem.

BELOW *Manuel I Comnenus was emperor of the Byzantines during the Second Crusade. He is shown on this gold Byzantine coin holding a sceptre and orb and with the hand of God crowning him.*

Hungary to the Danube and then through the Balkans. Louis's men proceeded in a relatively orderly fashion, their biggest problem being the procurement of food, since the larger German army had already consumed most of the available supplies.

THE GERMAN DEBACLE

While Louis was in the latter stages of his journey to Constantinople, Conrad crossed over from the city into Asia and marched his men to Nicaea. There he decided to split his force into two: one group, including most of the non-combatants, was to take the coast road to Attalia, while the main fighting force was to cross the interior of Anatolia. The decision, made contrary to Emperor Manuel's advice, led to disaster. Instead of waiting for Louis's troops to arrive, instead of keeping his own force intact, instead of leading his whole army along the coast road, which wound through Byzantine territory, Conrad committed a tactical folly.

As Conrad's main army approached Dorylaeum, where the knights of the First Crusade had scored a stunning victory over the Turks, the tables were now turned. On October 25, short of food and water and exhausted from marching in the relentless heat, the Germans were suddenly confronted by a Seljuk host. Overwhelmed, they were thrown into disorder and routed. Conrad and only a few others escaped to tell the tale back in Nicaea. Meanwhile, the other German group, unaware of the disaster that had befallen their comrades, marched along the Aegean coast road. Their progress was smooth until they turned inland and were attacked by Turks in Laodicea; the crushed remnant of the army was then attacked again in February 1148 in Pamphylia. Those few who survived managed to make it to Attalia, from where they sailed to Syria.

Louis and his troops, meanwhile, reached Constantinople in early October 1147, and toward the end of the month they began to hear rumours about the German crusaders. Only when the French crossed over to Asia and advanced to Nicaea did they learn directly about the debacle. Louis met with Conrad and what was left of his army, and the two kings decided to continue the crusade together, advancing by way of the coast road. All went well until they reached the city of Ephesus, the ancient port where St Paul lived and preached. At this point, Conrad fell ill and had to return to Constantinople, where he received the kindly ministrations of Emperor Manuel.

The leaderless Germans continued the slog to Syria with their French colleagues, both sets of soldiers growing weary from marching and the pressure of the lightning Turkish raids that picked off stragglers. A pitched battle ensued on January 1, 1148, at the bridge over the river beside Pisidian Antioch (not to be confused with Antioch in Syria). The crusaders eventually prevailed,

ABOVE *The crusading kings Louis VII and Conrad III arrive at Constantinople with great pomp in this 12th-century French illumination.*

but there then followed a grinding, hungry trek over mountains to Attalia. There, the town's Byzantine governor had to break the news to them that food stocks were low and the ships promised by the Byzantines were far too few to carry the whole army to Syria. The crusaders were forced to camp outside the city walls, where they were duly raided by the Turks. This naturally increased their resentment of the Greeks – indeed, some historians believe that Emperor Manuel, fearful of the French, was deliberately undermining their war effort. In the end, Louis and some hand-picked troops managed to sail off to Syria, followed shortly by the rest of the knights. The infantry had to make their way overland to Syria as best they could, a marathon that resulted in many fatalities from hunger, illness and Turkish attacks.

THE ROAD TO DAMASCUS

The crusaders' destination in Syria was Antioch, where, in March 1148, Louis and Eleanor were warmly welcomed by its ruler, Raymond, who also happened to be Eleanor's uncle. With the arrival of this new body of fighting men, the eyes of the Frankish leaders lit up. Raymond wanted the newcomers for himself, to counter the threat of Nur al-Din and specifically to attack Aleppo; the count of Edessa wanted them to help him restore his capital; and the count of Tripoli needed their manpower to recapture the strategic castle of Montferrand. Louis was indecisive at the best of times, and now he was being pulled in different directions. His mind was finally made up for him by his wife, Eleanor, who pleaded her uncle Raymond's cause so passionately that Louis began to suspect them of having an inappropriate relationship. So the king decided to leave for Jerusalem, dragging Eleanor with him, and there he was reunited with Conrad, who had recovered from his illness and made his way from Constantinople to Palestine by boat.

The question as to what the Franks should do with the forces at their disposal was still to be answered. To address it, Queen Melisende and her son King Baldwin III held a grand conference at Acre on June 24, 1148. Louis and Conrad sat round with all the leading Outremer barons, except Raymond and the count of Tripoli, to discuss the best way forward. Finally, it was decided to attack Damascus, a city that still maintained its biblical allure and whose capture would have been a feather in the cap for both Louis and Conrad. Historians down the ages have debated the wisdom of this decision, and some believe it was a recipe for disaster. For Damascus feared Nur al-Din as much as the Franks did; indeed, the city had made an alliance with Jerusalem against Aleppo in 1139. By attacking Damascus the Franks would surely push it into the gleeful arms of their erstwhile rival. On the other hand, there were good strategic reasons for capturing what was the largest city in Syria, thereby preventing the Muslims from uniting into a formidable force.

The crusaders' army, which, at an estimated 50,000 troops, was the largest yet to take the field, surrounded Damascus on July 24, 1148, and, perhaps inevitably, prompted the city's governor Unur to send a message to Nur al-Din for help. The Christians quickly captured the local orchards, which were infested with pockets of Damascene soldiers, and pressed threateningly against the southern walls. But then things began to go wrong. Muslim reinforcements started reaching the city via its northern gates, and the defenders launched a counterattack that cleared the crusaders away from their walls. Muslim guerrillas then infiltrated the orchards and, using the trees as cover, struck at the crusaders so effectively that the command was given to evacuate the position and move to an open plain to the east of the city, where the guerrillas would have no cover. But nor did the

la cité dunae . Cui la fondit. de fruitz et iardins asonuuon . De sordre que tinrent les princes a cassieger . Comment les iardins furent prins . Du grant coup que fit semperour . Et de la tru hifon pour laquelle fut le siege faite . la cité estant prest de prendre .

. lxvii .

Amae est la plu tyrant Cité de la terre de la mendre Gurre qui par autstre nom est apel see . La plaine de siban et a cesse ocrasion dit le prophete parlant de ceste Cité de damae Chief de Gurre . Cui des ser uiteurs de abraham apelle damae la fondit et fut par ce

crusaders and, what was worse, not only was no ready source of water but they now faced the most redoubtable fortifications of the city.

With Muslim reinforcements increasing and the imminent prospect of the arrival of Nur al-Din's army, the local Frankish barons realized the precariousness of their position and advised Louis and Conrad to retreat. Although both were dismayed by what they considered to be the Franks' lack of commitment to the cause, in the end they had no choice. On July 28, the crusaders began the slow march back to Galilee, harassed by Turkish light cavalry, and thence to Jerusalem. The vast sums of money, the elaborate preparations, the long, gruelling journeys and bloody encounters with the enemy had ended in a humiliating catastrophe.

Conrad left the Holy Land on September 8, 1148, and recuperated at the court of Manuel in Constantinople. The marriage of his brother, Henry, to Manuel's niece Theodora cheered his spirits, as did the prospect of an alliance between himself and Manuel against the dangerous Norman, King Roger of Sicily.

Louis lingered on in Palestine until the following year. Learning of Conrad's pact with Manuel, he decided to ally himself with Roger and sailed off in a Sicilian ship in the summer of 1149, eventually making his way to the Sicilian king. The latter welcomed his royal guest and soon suggested that they should lead a crusade against the Byzantines. Bitter about various experiences during the crusade which he construed to be instances of Byzantine treachery, Louis readily agreed to the plan. He then enlisted heavyweight churchmen, including Bernard of Clairvaux, to preach against the Byzantines. But Pope Eugenius was not eager to attack his fellow Christians, and Conrad, of course, now had a close relationship with Manuel. Without those two key players the crusade was a non-starter. The idea was dropped, only to re-emerge half a century later.

ABOVE *Christian archers and crossbowmen exchange fire with their Muslim counterparts across the Barada River near the walls of Damascus in this 15th-century French illumination.*

Miles famosus Rex Ricardus generosus
Non hominem metuit, tantus ad arma fuit

Rodolor o mortis, mundo pressio fortis

4

THE GREAT ADVERSARIES

The Third Crusade (1189-92), prompted by the Muslims' recapture of Jerusalem in 1187, was notable for bringing together on the field of conflict two of the great adversaries of the crusading period: Richard I, the Lionheart, king of England, one of the most brilliant generals of the Middle Ages, and Sultan Salah al-Din Yusuf, better known as Saladin, the foremost Muslim leader of his time. Both men were brave, shrewd, charismatic commanders, perfectly suited for the stage of war on which history had placed them. By the start of the crusade Richard was in his early 30s and at the height of his considerable physical powers. Tall, fair-haired, strongly built, he was renowned for his courage and energy as well as for his charm and his delight in the arts of music and verse. His defects were his vanity and volcanic temper: when the red mist descended he was capable of savage cruelty, as when he had more than 2,500 Muslim prisoners massacred in cold blood after the siege of Acre in July 1191. Yet his dashing appearance and heroic deeds were the stuff of legend and, after his death, they were perpetuated in the poems and songs of troubadours and poets in England, France and other parts of Europe. Even the Muslims had respect for this tawny-haired giant, whom they called Malik Ric.

BELOW *This joust between Christian and Muslim knights from the 14th-century Luttrell Psalter is usually thought to represent Richard the Lionheart and Saladin, depicted with a malevolent blue face.*

About 20 years older and less physically imposing than his Christian foe, Saladin was none the less Richard's peer in determination, energy and bravery and his master in chivalry and long-term campaign strategy. A gifted Kurdish soldier, Saladin rose to become vizier of Egypt in 1169. Five years later he was able to proclaim himself the sultan of Syria and Egypt, and for the next decade he extended and consolidated his empire. He was a devout Muslim and enjoyed nothing more than listening to theological debates by scholars. Renowned for his generosity, he is said to have looked on "money as one looks on the dust in the road", and he gave much of it to charitable causes. His name became a byword for chivalry. One time, when he was besieging the crusader castle of Kerak, east of the Dead Sea, he ordered his mangonels (siege engines) to refrain from hurling rocks at a particular tower because it was the bridal suite of a recently-married Christian couple. On another occasion, he was so moved by Richard's courage during a battle that when the king's horse was killed from under him he ordered two fresh steeds to be taken to him under a flag of truce.

THE AFTERMATH OF DISASTER

After the disaster of the inconsequential Second Crusade, many in the west began to regard crusader ideology in a less favourable light. From 1150 to 1185 papal attempts to stir the faithful to take the cross – in reply to requests for help from the Franks in the east – met with a limited response. Part of the problem was that the kings of England and France, Henry II and Louis VII, who would be crucial to any substantial crusade, were at war with each other, and neither man was willing to set off to Palestine leaving his rival behind.

Meanwhile, in the Latin east, the crusaders' failure at Damascus had left the Muslims in Syria, under Nur al-Din, more united and stronger than ever, especially after the latter occupied Damascus in 1154. With the menacing shadow of Nur al-Din cast over them, the Franks decided

ABOVE
Saladin's status as a legendary warrior was established in both the Muslim and Christian worlds, as is shown in this late medieval Christian portrayal of him wielding a scimitar.

to try to strengthen their position by basing a strategic policy around the Shiite Fatimid caliphate of Egypt, the traditional rival of the Sunni caliphs of Baghdad. In fact Fatimid politics at this time were descending into chaos, if not farce, as viziers – the actual rulers of the country, the caliphs being the religious and ceremonial leaders – came and went in a mêlée of revolts and murders. The resulting power vacuum sucked in the interest of both Nur al-Din and the Christian king of Jerusalem, Amalric I (1163–74), who was to invade Egypt five times in seven years.

In 1164 Nur al-Din himself sent an army to Egypt under a Kurdish general named Shirkuh, accompanied by his nephew Saladin, to install a man called Shawar as vizier, in return for the latter's support and loyalty. But, once he was in power, Shawar reneged on his deal with Nur al-Din and invited Amalric to come and fight his cause. In the following years the struggle between Amalric and Shirkuh slid into a stalemate. Finally the impasse was ended when Shirkuh himself was invited by the Egyptians to become vizier. He accepted the offer, but died a few weeks later. His place was taken by his nephew: in March 1169, at the age of 31, Saladin found himself vizier of Egypt, ruling it on behalf of Nur al-Din.

Egypt's new ruler consolidated his power base and in September 1171, after the death of the Fatimid caliph, he transferred the country's allegiance to the caliph of Baghdad, thereby bringing it into the Sunni fold. One result of this was to push the small but influential Shiite sect known as the Assassins, now deprived of support from formerly Shiite Egypt, into making an alliance with the Franks.

As time passed, Nur al-Din began to fret about Saladin, whose reassurances of loyalty were not always matched by his actions. The tension between master and subordinate, however, was resolved in 1174, when Nur al-Din died, igniting a power struggle in Syria. In the same year Amalric also died, and from the resultant succession crisis his 13-year-old son – who was not only too young to rule but also a leper – was crowned Baldwin IV. A regent was needed to be found quickly, and Count Raymond III of Tripoli was appointed for three years until the king came of age.

While Muslim Syria and the kingdom of Jerusalem were trying to restore a semblance of stability, it was the turn of the

THE ASSASSINS

One of the most influential and dangerous Muslim groups relative to their small size, the Assassins were an Ismaili or Sevener Shiite sect. They became known for the ruthless efficiency with which they dispatched their political enemies in cold blood – whether Muslims or Christians. Their name is said to derive from "hashshāshin", the drug which it was claimed they took to help them in their deadly work. The Assassins' high-profile victims included Conrad of Montferrat, while both Saladin and Nur al-Din only just managed to survive their attacks.

The founder of the sect was a Persian Shiite named Hasan ibn Sabah, who was born in about 1048. During his early 20s, Hasan decided to move to Shiite-dominated Egypt to escape the orthodox Sunni regime established by the Seljuk Turks after their conquest of the greater part of the Near East. Then, in 1090, Hasan left Egypt and made his headquarters in the fortress of Alamut in the Elburz Mountains by the Caspian Sea. There, as grand master of the sect, he set about organizing and instilling discipline and absolute loyalty into his followers. His most potent weapon was murder: he would commission an individual or a group of two or three people to target a particular person. The agents would typically disguise themselves as, say, traders, and live for a while in the place where they were to execute their victim, plotting his habits and movements. Murders were committed in public to maximize publicity and spread fear – the murderers were resigned to being caught and executed, but their self-sacrifice added to the sect's mystique. Naturally enough, the Assassins were feared and loathed throughout the Muslim world, and there were sometimes violent reactions to them. In 1113 in Aleppo in Syria, where many Assassins had settled and their influence was strong, the city's authorities suddenly rounded them up and executed them. The same thing happened in Damascus in 1129.

Of the sect's later leaders, perhaps the best known was Rashid al-Din, "the Old Man of the Mountains", who directed operations from the stronghold of Masyaf in Syria. Rashi was a political pragmatist, demonstrated by the fact that he was prepared to ally himself with the Christian king Amalric of Jerusalem against his co-religionist Nur al-Din. He remained leader for nearly 30 years, surviving a determined push by Saladin (himself a survivor of an attempted assassination) to clear the sect from the Syrian mountains in 1176. The Assassins were virtually wiped out in Iran by the Mongols in the mid-thirteenth century, and they were dispersed in Syria by the Mamluk sultan Baybars in the 1270s.

Byzantine Empire to suffer a disaster. In 1176 Emperor Manuel confronted the Seljuk Turks under Kilij Arslan II at Myriocephalum near Pisidian Antioch in Anatolia and his huge army was destroyed. The catastrophe was as great as the Byzantines' defeat by the Turks at Manzikert a century before, and it made the long-term future of the empire extremely bleak.

THE RISE OF SALADIN

With the Christians in the east in disarray and after the dissolution of Nur al-Din's empire, Saladin was presented with a golden opportunity to make himself the undisputed master of the region. At first he concentrated mainly on the Muslim states of Syria and, although he did not always have matters his own way, Damascus capitulated to him in 1174, Aleppo in 1183 and Mosul in 1186. With Muslim Syria secure, he could now turn his whole attention to the Christians.

While Saladin was patiently accumulating power, the kingdom of Jerusalem continued to be racked with political uncertainty, which revolved around the decline and imminent death of Baldwin. As his health began to fail, the jockeying for power intensified and centred on two individuals: the regent, Raymond of Tripoli, who had the support of the Outremer barons and the leper king himself; and Guy of Lusignan, a handsome young Frenchman who had married Baldwin's sister, Sibylla. The infighting finally came to a head after the king died in 1185. His child successor lasted only 18 months before he died too, at which point Sibylla spotted her chance and had herself and Guy quickly crowned king and queen of Jerusalem. Trumped, Raymond and his supporters had to accept this *fait accompli*.

Not long after the coronation, a truce which had been made between Saladin and the Franks in 1185 was broken by a devil-may-care Frankish noble named Reynald of Châtillon, whose continual reckless and selfish actions and cruelty were abhorred by friends and foes alike. After Reynald attacked a Muslim caravan journeying from Egypt to Damascus, Saladin demanded compensation. When this was denied to him, he fatefully declared war. Crossing the River Jordan on June 30, 1187, Saladin attacked the town of Tiberias in Galilee on July 2, overcame its outer defences and besieged the citadel. Despite warnings from Raymond of Tripoli not to risk going to the citadel's aid (even though his own wife was trapped there), King Guy assembled a large force and marched

RIGHT *The hill known as the Horns of Hattin in Galilee was the scene of King Guy of Jerusalem's fateful defeat by Saladin in July, 1187. Three months later Jerusalem itself fell to the Muslims.*

north. On July 4, in the burning summer heat, the tired and thirsty Christian force found themselves surrounded near the twin-peaked hill known as the Horns of Hattin. Decimated by showers of arrows loosed by the Muslim light cavalry, the Frankish force crumpled and was routed. King Guy and some of his nobles surrendered, but almost the entire army was killed or sold into slavery.

The defeat at Hattin was a complete disaster for the Franks: it was only a matter of time before almost all of the kingdom's other towns and castles, deprived of any potential relief force, surrendered to Saladin, culminating with Jerusalem itself on October 2, 1187, after a two-week siege. Only the port of Tyre in the south and Tripoli and Antioch in the north along with a sprinkling of castles still flew the Franks' flags. The kingdom of Jerusalem was on its knees. Its only hope of salvation lay in a fresh crusade from Europe.

ABOVE *Muslim troops under Saladin storm Jerusalem in this medieval illumination. Saladin's merciful treatment of captives was in stark contrast to the behaviour of the crusaders after their capture of the city in 1099.*

THE WESTERN RIPOSTE

With the fall of the Holy City to Saladin – the news of which is said to have sent Pope Urban III to an early grave – the west at last roused itself from its apathy. The new pope, Gregory VIII, issued an encyclical that attributed the disaster in the east to the sins of all Christians and called for penance and a recourse to arms against the enemy. Eventually the warring kings of England and France, Henry and Philip (Louis VII's successor), agreed to a truce and took the cross, and both raised money for the crusade with a tax known as the Saladin tithe.

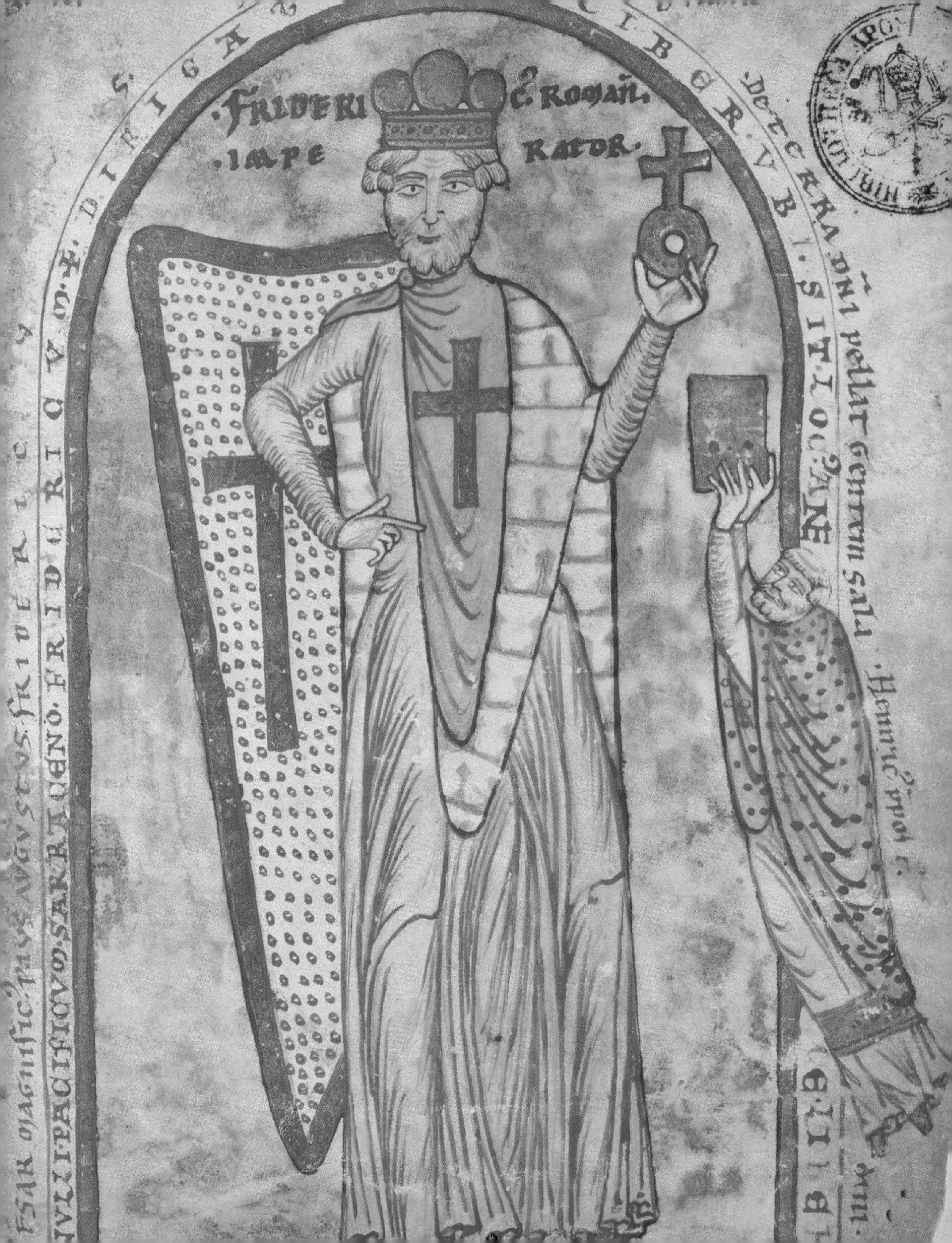

·FRIDERI C. ROMAN
·IMPE RATOR

Although Henry died in July 1189, his son Richard I, nature's gift to warfare, was crowned king of England and took his father's place on the imminent expedition, in which he was to be the driving force.

Richard and Philip were by no means the only stars of this latest war effort. The elderly but still mightily impressive German emperor, Frederick I, Barbarossa, probably the most revered statesman in Europe, amassed a huge army (probably half the size of the 100,000-strong force claimed by chroniclers but still probably the largest ever single crusading army). Leaving Regensburg in May 1189, the Germans journeyed through Hungary uneventfully but, as had so often happened in the past, encountered trouble in Byzantine territories, where they were attacked by brigands. They also received little or no cooperation from the Byzantine emperor, the elderly Isaac II, Angelus, who was nervous at reports of a vast western host advancing toward him. It was probably with great relief that, in February 1190, Isaac arranged for Frederick to cross the Dardanelles near Gallipoli into Asia, thereby bypassing Constantinople.

Like previous crusaders, Frederick's men suffered from heat and exhaustion as they marched across Anatolia, as well as from attacks by the Turks. On May 18, 1190, the Germans fought off a determined Turkish assault near Iconium (modern Konya). Buoyant from this victory, they continued their journey eastward, crossing the Taurus Mountains into Cilicia. But at the River Calycadnus (Göksu) near the town of Seleucia disaster struck: while swimming in the river, Emperor Frederick drowned – no one knows how, but he might have suffered a heart attack – and with him sank, in an instant, the aspirations and morale of his loyal German troops. Bereft and leaderless, many men returned home straightaway. Some sailed to the Holy Land, while others, under Frederick's son, the duke of Swabia, marched overland, braving the elements and Turkish raids, and taking with them Frederick's corpse, pickled in vinegar. When the sorry remnants of the German host arrived in Antioch their priority was to inter their decomposing emperor in St Peter's Cathedral.

ABOVE *Philip II, Augustus, one of the leaders of the Third Crusade, is crowned king of France at Rheims Cathedral in this medieval French illumination.*

SHIPWRECK AND SIEGE

Yet even though the German contribution to the crusade had come to little, the Franks of the Latin east still invested hope in the armies of Richard and Philip. The French and English kings marched off together with their respective forces from Vézelay on July 4, 1190. They then diverged at Lyons before meeting up again on the island of Sicily, where they wintered. Richard became embroiled in local politics, which involved the maltreatment of his sister Joanna, who had been married to the late king of Sicily but was now suffering at the hands of his successor. After a convincing show of force by Richard, the problems were soon ironed out.

In March 1191, Philip sailed off for Palestine, with Richard following in early April. The latter made an unscheduled stop on the island of Cyprus – blown there by a storm – where the self-styled Byzantine governor, a usurper named Isaac, was foolish enough to pick a fight with him, refusing

OPPOSITE *Emperor Frederick I, Barbarossa, tragically drowned in a river in Anatolia while leading his German host to the Holy Land. Here he is shown dressed as a crusader knight.*

to hand back to the king a number of shipwrecked sailors and valuables rescued from the sea. Richard responded by overwhelming the Cypriot garrison and capturing the whole island.

Richard then set sail for Palestine and in June arrived off the coast of Muslim-held Acre, which for two years had been under siege by a Christian force led by King Guy, the homeless ruler of Jerusalem. How had this situation come about? After the battle of Hattin, Saladin had taken Guy captive but later released him on condition that he swore not to fight against the Muslims again. As soon as he was free, Guy had been absolved of his oath by the church, on the basis that he had made it to a Muslim. Then in 1188, eager to regain his power, Guy had made his way to Tyre, where most of the Christian refugees had gathered. But his attempts to enter the city failed. Conrad of Montferrat, whose courage, swift decision-making and good organization had saved Tyre from falling into Saladin's hands, refused to receive Guy as king, believing that he had forfeited his right to the crown by his defeat at Hattin and imprisonment. The choice of king should be decided by the leaders of the new crusade.

ABOVE *Powerful Christian knights capture the city of Acre in July 1191, while turbaned Muslim defenders offer their submission.*

In April 1189, Guy tried again to persuade Conrad to hand Tyre over to him but without success. Frustrated, and feeling the need to demonstrate his kingly authority, Guy marched south with a small force to besiege Acre. On the face of it, this was an act of folly – the Muslim defenders outnumbered Guy's men by two to one, and the field army of Saladin could turn up at any moment. But Guy was determined and courageous, and even though his assault on the city failed, he camped below its walls and waited for reinforcements to come. Saladin reacted by surrounding Guy's position, but he was unable to penetrate it. As time passed, Guy grew stronger as soldiers who had survived Hattin, visiting knights from Europe and German contingents from Emperor Frederick's army arrived to swell his forces. The coming of King Philip and the French on April 20, 1191, boosted morale further. When Richard turned up with a fleet of 25 ships, there was at last a confidence that the stalemate could be broken.

But the prosecution of the siege was not easy. Richard, whose standing and innate authority made him the natural leader of the combined Christian forces, fell ill – although even in his sickness he was more effective than the cautious and relatively inexperienced Philip, who was still only in his mid-20s. Nevertheless, the French king had had the foresight to construct formidable siege weapons, including a great catapult nicknamed "The Neighbour from Hell", and these continued to pound Acre's walls, smashing stone and creating gaps which the defenders hurried to plug, while Saladin tried to mount diversionary attacks. For the Christians, there was also the distraction of internal frictions. Bad blood existed between Richard and Philip over rival territorial claims (especially in France, where Richard had inherited vast domains). Each man took sides in the local power struggle for the right to rule the kingdom of Jerusalem between Guy and Conrad of Montferrat, with Richard backing Guy (who was his vassal in France) and Philip Conrad (who was his cousin).

In the end, the naval blockade by the English made the crucial difference. The defenders' food was fast running out and they became desperate. On July 7, they sent a swimmer out to make contact with Saladin and tell him they would have to surrender unless he helped them immediately. Before Saladin could react, however, Acre capitulated. In return for their lives the Muslims agreed to hand over the city intact to the crusaders along with 200,000 gold pieces, the relic of the True Cross, which Saladin had captured at Hattin, and the release of 1,500 Christian rank-and-file prisoners as well as 100 nobles. Richard took the precaution of holding some 2,700 Muslim prisoners to ensure the conditions were met.

A LIMITED ADVANCE

After the majority of the Acre garrison had left – to the grudging respect of the Christians – the crusaders entered the city and began to make themselves at home, and to quarrel. In one fateful incident, Leopold, duke of Austria, placed his standard next to that of Richard – too presumptuously close in the eyes of some English soldiers, who tore it from the wall and threw it in the dry moat below. Leopold would later gain satisfaction for this insult. There was also, still, the contentious issue of who should rule the Latin kingdom – Guy or Conrad? In the end a compromise was reached: Guy should reign during his lifetime then, on his death, the crown should pass to Conrad (whose wife was the half-sister of Guy's wife) and his descendants.

The group dynamic of the crusaders' high command improved considerably when King Philip decided he had had enough of the campaign and left for Europe on July 31, leaving Richard – who was nervous of the mischief Philip might cause back home – the undisputed leader of the army. Richard began this new phase of the crusade with an act of savagery. A wrangle with Saladin over the fulfilment of the terms of Acre's surrender prompted the English king to have his Muslim hostages butchered in cold blood in sight of the Muslim army encamped nearby. This act was thrown into stark relief by the clemency Saladin typically (but not always) showed after victories over the Christians. The English king then decided to march to Jerusalem and led his men south from Acre via the coast road, his right flank covered by the English ships, moving slowly in tandem just offshore. Saladin and his forces remained inland, tracking the crusaders, waiting for a suitable opportunity to force battle.

Saladin decided to attack the Christians on September 7, 1191, at Arsuf, several miles north of Jaffa, where he ordered his troops to spread out across the coastal plain. Richard drew up his smaller, but heavier armed, force of knights and infantry into a close formation opposite Saladin and waited for his opponent to make the first move. As the morning sun began to climb the Muslims suddenly made the first of several charges against the Christian line, but again and again they were repelled by the armour-clad knights and the lethal arrows of the bowmen. As Richard waited patiently to make a decisive counter-thrust, two Hospitallers broke rank and charged the enemy, prompting their comrades to follow suit. Seeing that the Christians were now committed to the offensive Richard himself galloped forth, taking control of the attack. Unable to withstand the ferocity and weight of the crusaders' assault, the Muslims fled the field or died bravely where they stood. It was a magnificent triumph for Richard and one that dimmed the aura of invincibility that Saladin had acquired in Christian minds.

Yet the victory was by no means decisive, and any strategic advantage the Christians had gained soon evaporated. Saladin's losses turned out to be not as grave as he had feared. And the crusaders, for their part, were exhausted from the constant fighting and marching. So instead of pressing on to Jerusalem, Richard allowed his weary army to have some well-earned rest and recreation among the fleshpots of Jaffa. Before long he came to realize that his resources were not strong enough to sustain his advance and that it would be best to make peace with the enemy on favourable terms while he still had the military advantage. So he broached the possibility of a truce with Saladin, who agreed to consider it.

DIPLOMATIC RELATIONS

The negotiations carried on for about a year and revolved around meetings between Richard and Saladin's brother al-Adil, who grew to respect and like each other. Indeed, the English king even suggested that al-Adil should marry his sister, Joanna, and together preside at Jerusalem. Whether this was a serious proposal or a pipe-dream of Richard's, it was a non-starter. Joanna was shocked at the idea of marrying a Muslim; al-Adil politely declined the opportunity to become a Christian (a condition of the marriage); and Saladin, believing Richard's suggestion was an example of the Frankish sense of humour, played along with the "joke" and pretended to agree to it. If Richard felt let down, he was partially compensated by a splendid feast held in his honour by al-Adil on November 8, 1191, where gifts and words of mutual affection were exchanged.

However, the two sides were no nearer to a peace deal. As winter began to set in, Saladin discharged a large part of his army and retired to Jerusalem. Richard refused to be deterred by the onset of rain and freezing weather and decided to make an assault on the Holy City. By January 3, 1192, he and his army of Anglo-Norman and French crusaders (the latter left behind by Philip and led by the duke of Burgundy) were camped at Beit Nuba, only about 12 miles (19 km) away from Jerusalem. But the final push never came. Richard was persuaded by the local Christian barons that the bad weather, the city's walls and the threat of a Muslim relief force from Egypt all added up to an obstacle too great to be surmounted. Reluctantly, Richard retreated to Ascalon on the coast, where he set his disconsolate men the task of rebuilding the walls that Saladin had previously dismantled.

Richard then found himself intervening in local Outremer politics. The dispute between Guy and Conrad concerning the kingship of Jerusalem was still rumbling on and Richard, now becoming anxious to leave Palestine to attend to his affairs in England and France, was keen to sort it out before he left. Although he personally favoured Guy, his vassal, he found that the Frankish barons overwhelmingly supported Conrad, so he decided to change sides and back the latter. The agreement he brokered meant that Guy would become king of Cyprus and Conrad king of Jerusalem – a compromise that all concerned accepted. But the collective sigh of relief came too soon. On April 28, 1192, Conrad was murdered by two Assassins, apparently in revenge for an injury Conrad had once inflicted on the sect – although some pointed the finger at Richard himself – and the succession crisis reared up again. Fortunately, however, Conrad's widow quickly married Henry of Troyes, count of Champagne, who was the nephew of both Richard and Philip, and husband and wife became the titular heads of Jerusalem.

RETURN TO BATTLE

Having played the part of diplomat, Richard returned to his first love – fighting. On May 25 he captured the Muslim port of Daron, south of Gaza, and this success created the momentum that persuaded him to try his luck with Jerusalem again. On June 7 the Christian forces marched out of Ascalon and, four days later, reached Beit Nuba, the position they had occupied during the last failed attempt on the city. Yet again the expedition stalled. The fact was that Richard simply did not have enough supplies, equipment, manpower and time to mount a sustained campaign, and he was a wise enough soldier not to let the mirage of the Holy City tempt him into a disaster. And it was a real enough temptation: it is said that one day while reconnoitring the terrain he suddenly saw from a hill a vista of Jerusalem and quickly covered his eyes with his shield, feeling unworthy to gaze on the city which still remained beyond his grasp.

Richard remained camped near Jerusalem for about a month before ordering the retreat – the capture of a richly laden Muslim caravan was scant compensation for the disappointment his

soldiers felt. Back in Jaffa, still fretting to return home, Richard again started peace negotiations with Saladin. But the talks broke down over Ascalon, which Saladin would not countenance remaining a Christian port. Frustrated by the lack of progress, Richard decided he could not delay much longer and moved from Jaffa to Acre, ready to sail when some sort of agreement had been reached. On hearing of Richard's departure, Saladin, still full of fight, suddenly launched a surprise attack on Jaffa on July 27 and nearly succeeded in taking it. In the nick of time, Richard sailed back from Acre, leapt ashore at the head of a small band of troops and reinvigorated the Christian garrison – on the point of surrendering to Saladin – successfully turning the battle.

Richard's stay in the Holy Land may have been coming to an end, but he was determined to leave with a bang not a whimper, and only a week after his success at Jaffa he fought his last battle

ABOVE *The walls of Jerusalem remained beyond the grasp of Richard the Lionheart, who could not even bear to gaze upon them while the city was in Muslim hands.*

THE TEUTONIC KNIGHTS

Along with the Templars and Hospitallers, the Order of the Teutonic Knights was born in the Holy Land and gained considerable renown for its discipline and fighting ability. Distinguished by their white cloaks and black crosses, the knights not only fought in Palestine but also went on to conquer a vast territory in northern Europe that included parts of Russia, Lithuania, Prussia and much of the Baltic coast.

By the late twelfth century, a hospital founded by pious German merchants, dedicated to St Mary and intended for German pilgrims, had been established in Acre – similar to the Hospitaller foundation in Jerusalem. After the failure of Henry VI's crusade, a number of German knights decided to remain in the Holy Land, and their association with the hospital resulted in the founding of the Teutonic Order in 1198. Granted a tower over one of Acre's gates, the order soon received lands and castles in Syria and Europe. In the early thirteenth century they expanded their horizons to eastern Europe, where, in Poland, they fought pagan tribes in the name of Christ. They went on to gain control of Prussia and form an alliance with the Swordbrethren, a German order of knights, who were powerful in the eastern Baltic. But in 1242 they suffered a severe reversal in Russia when, in trying to capture the city of Novgorod, they faced the troops of Prince Alexander Nevsky on the frozen waters of Lake Peipus and were routed. Their defeat terminated their hopes of expansion into Russia.

By 1308, the year they based their headquarters at Marienburg, the Teutonic Knights controlled vast tracts of Germany and north-eastern Europe. In the following years, they concentrated their efforts on expanding their power in pagan Lithuania. Eventually, in 1386–87, Lithuania became united with Poland and embraced Catholicism in the process. In 1410 the combined Polish-Lithuanian forces defeated the knights decisively at Tannenberg. From now on, the knights' power and influence was on the wane, and the order was secularized in 1561.

ABOVE *A Teutonic knight returns from a crusade in this painting by the 19th-century Romantic German artist Karl Friedrich Lessing.*

against his great adversary. Since the Christians camped outside Jaffa were few in number, Saladin decided to attack them before they could be reinforced. But Richard was alerted to the impending assault only hours before it occurred and prepared his men accordingly. The Muslim cavalry charged but was unable to penetrate the Christian ranks, who won the day. It was while watching and admiring Richard's heroic fighting that Saladin sent him two horses during the thick of battle to replace the mount the English king had lost.

Richard's last victory was a fitting end to his crusade, which, however, had failed to recapture Jerusalem. According to the five-year peace treaty finally agreed by Richard and Saladin, the Christians were allowed to keep the Palestinian ports as far south as Jaffa, except Ascalon, and Christian pilgrims were permitted free access to Jerusalem and other holy places. Although it was the best Richard could do, the terms were ultimately poor recompense for the effort and money which had been poured into the crusade by Europe's greatest rulers but that had left Jerusalem in Muslim hands.

FALLEN HEROES

Richard left Palestine on October 9, 1192. Within six months Saladin was dead. Worn out by years of campaigning, and suffering from ill health, Saladin retired to Damascus on November 4, 1192. There he began to show signs of uncharacteristic lethargy and, in the following months, succumbed to a painful fever. By March 1, 1193, he was bed-ridden and beginning to decline rapidly. Two days later, as the words "There is no God but He; in Him I place my trust" were being read to him from the Qur'ān he stirred then quietly passed away.

At the time his erstwhile opponent died, Richard was languishing in prison. His voyage from the Holy Land ended in a shipwreck off the Italian coast, from where he set out overland to England. In Austria, however, he was taken prisoner in December 1192 by Duke Leopold, whose banner Richard's men had torn down at Acre. Leopold then handed Richard over to the German emperor, Henry VI, who released him in February 1194 only after the payment of a massive ransom (both Leopold and Henry were cousins of the assassinated Conrad of Montferrat, and it is possible they believed Richard was to blame for his death). For the next five years Richard defended his territories in France before succumbing to an arrow wound on April 11, 1199.

Richard's captor, Emperor Henry VI, was involved in a coda to the Third Crusade, often known as the German Crusade. The son of Frederick Barbarossa, Henry wanted to expand German influence and gain the international prestige in the east that his father had failed to achieve. Accordingly, he raised a huge army which he sent over to Palestine in September 1197. Having occupied Sidon and Beirut, the Germans marched through Galilee, hoping to make an assault on Jerusalem. But their siege of the castle of Toron got bogged down. They then heard the distressing news of the death of their emperor at Messina in Sicily. Fearing imminent unrest in Germany, they quickly retreated to Tyre, from where they set sail for home a few days later. The venture had been a failure; but the presence of German crusaders in the Holy Land at this time did give rise to the third of the great medieval military orders, the Teutonic Knights (see Box).

RIGHT *An anxious-looking King Richard is arrested in Vienna on his way back from the Third Crusade in this late 13th-century English illumination.*

BELOW *After his death in 1199, Richard was buried at Fontevraud Abbey in France beside his mother Eleanor of Aquitaine (holding a book) and other members of the Plantagenet family.*

STRIKING AT THE EMPIRE

In the late twelfth century and early years of the thirteenth, the crusading spirit in Europe was promoted and fortified by Innocent III, one of the greatest popes of the Middle Ages. The most dramatic result of his efforts was the Fourth Crusade, planned as an invasion of Egypt, which, after the death of Saladin, was considered to be the most vulnerable spot in the Muslim empire. Instead, however, the campaign ended in Latin Catholic Christians killing Greek Orthodox Christians and the brutal sacking and pillaging of Constantinople, the greatest city in Christendom. The crusade shocked Europe and left a bitter memory in the minds of Greeks, which even now has yet to be expunged. How did this extraordinary situation come about?

MUSTERING THE FORCES

After the failures of the Third Crusade and Emperor Henry VI's German Crusade, the momentum for a new expedition to the east was generated by Innocent himself. A noble-born Roman who never doubted the supremacy of the church, Innocent was elected pope in 1198. The 18 years of his reign were to see not only a major crusade being preached against the church's enemies abroad but also expeditions launched against those closer to home, especially the heretical Albigensians of southern France . The pope's enthusiasm for crusading was part of a larger reform programme that saw him play a crucial role in supporting the new mendicant orders of the Franciscans and Dominicans, as well as presiding over the important Fourth Lateran Council in 1215. His eagerness to provide military assistance to the east stemmed partly from wanting to help the Latin kingdom of Jerusalem, and partly from wishing to consolidate the religious authority of Rome in Palestine.

Determined to keep the direction of any new crusade as much as possible under his control, Innocent issued an encyclical in 1198, which aimed his appeal not so much at Europe's monarchs – most of whom were anyway preoccupied with domestic concerns – but at the continent's leading nobles, who would be more likely to accept the spiritual leadership of the see of Rome. At first, however, Europe's aristocrats were generally tepid about his call to arms. There was greater enthusiasm among the common people, largely owing to the rhetoric of the itinerant preacher Fulk of Neuilly, who travelled around France, stirring up interest. Eventually, in November 1199, the first two "big names" joined the cause: Count Thibald III of Champagne, a nephew of King Philip Augustus of France and King Richard the Lionheart of England, and Count Louis of Blois. In the following weeks more nobles took the cross and plans were discussed. It seems that a consensus was gradually reached that Egypt should be the crusade's objective, not least because King Richard himself had identified the country as being the weak link in the Muslims' defences.

As initial preparations for the expedition began to get under way, a major logistical problem presented itself: how would the crusaders journey to Egypt? The land route across Anatolia to Syria was now too dangerous, which left travel by ship as the sole option. The only problem was that none of the crusaders had the sort of kingly wealth to build and finance a fleet. So an approach was made to the powerful maritime republic of Venice.

NEGOTIATIONS AND AGREEMENTS

A delegation sent by the crusaders arrived in Venice in February 1201 and talks were held with the republic's authorities, led by the semi-blind but sprightly octogenarian doge ("duke"), Enrico Dandolo, a man who was as sharp as he was wily and daring. The two parties clinched a deal: in return for Venice supplying enough ships to convey 4,500 knights, 9,000 squires, 20,000 foot-soldiers and nine months' provisions, the crusaders would pay 85,000 silver marks. The Venetians also offered to provide an extra 50 ships at their own expense in return for half of the crusade's spoils. That Egypt was the agreed destination was kept quiet, for it was felt it

THE ALBIGENSIAN CRUSADE

The idea of the crusade is often associated exclusively with the great Christian expeditions to the east to fight the Muslims. There were also, however, crusades aimed at Muslims in the Iberian peninsula, pagans in the Baltic and elsewhere, and heretics. Of the expeditions against the latter, the Albigensian Crusade, which was initiated by Pope Innocent III and took place shortly after the sack of Constantinople, is probably the best known and most important.

The Albigenses, who took their name from the town of Albi in Languedoc in southern France, were a branch of the Cathars, a sect thought to originate from Bulgaria. The Cathars were dualists, who held that in the universe there were two eternal principles of good and evil. Everything material was considered evil, while spiritual things were good. This train of thought led them to deeply heretical views about the incarnation, passion and resurrection of Christ. For they believed that Christ could not have become a flesh-and-blood man (flesh being material and therefore evil) but had lived as an insubstantial phantom. He had not suffered and died on the cross, nor had he been raised from the dead.

If the Albigenses had been known purely for their theology then they probably would not have gained much popularity. What made them attractive was the way they conducted their lives. The sect was split into two groups, the *perfecti* ("perfect") and *credentes* ("believers"). The latter lived ordinary lives but were supposed to receive what was known as the *consolamentum*, an act of absolution conveyed by a laying on of hands, once before they died. After this they had to live like one of the perfects, who had higher moral standards and were celibate and rigorous vegetarians (the idea being to distance themselves from the evil material world). The vivid contrast between the ascetic, pious perfects and the relatively lax local Catholic priests helped to draw many ordinary people to the sect, which also gained recruits or at least sympathy from among the nobles.

By the latter half of the twelfth century, the church was well aware of the danger the heretics of Languedoc posed. Papal envoys were sent to preach to them in 1198 and 1203 but without success; a couple of years later St Dominic, founder of the Dominicans, also tried to make headway. But in 1208, after the assassination of the papal legate Peter of Castelnau – probably by someone in the household of Raymond VI of Toulouse – Pope Innocent III's patience snapped and he launched a crusade against the Albigenses. Key to Innocent's strategy was land: the crusaders, drawn mostly from the north of France, were to be allowed to keep any

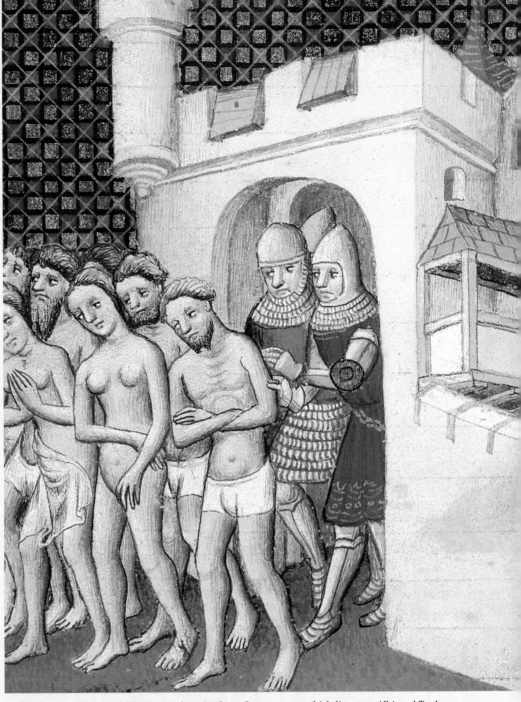

ABOVE *Crusaders expel Albigensian heretics from Carcassonne, which lies near Albi and Toulouse, the heartland of the heresy. The town capitulated in 1209 and its citizens were allowed to leave with "nothing but their sins".*

land they won from the Cathar heretics or their sympathizers. There were also geo-political interests: backing the crusaders and their leader Simon de Montfort (the elder) was the king of France, eager to expand his domain, while Raymond of Toulouse was supported by Peter II of Aragon.

The crusaders' first target was the town of Béziers, where in July 1209 its Cathar and Catholic citizens fought shoulder to shoulder to save their homes, but in vain. As the crusaders stormed the walls, the terrified defenders took refuge in a church, where they were burnt to death. When the papal legate was told that not only Cathars but

Catholics were dying in the flames, he is said to have commented: "Kill them all, God will know his own."

The crusaders won another decisive victory at Muret in 1213, but the war continued to drag on. It finally ended with the Peace of Paris in 1229, the terms of which gave the French king Louis IX possession of the county of Toulouse. But it was only after the founding of the Inquisition by Pope Gregory IX in 1231 – it was established in Toulouse two years later – and a systematic and prolonged sweep of Languedoc by Dominican inquisitors that Catharism was finally extirpated.

might deter some of the crusaders, for whom the mystique of the Holy Land was the motive force behind their joining the expedition.

Soon after the crusaders and the Venetians had concluded their deal, Thibald of Champagne died, and his place as leader was taken by Marquis Boniface of Montferrat. During the rest of 1201 the crusaders prepared themselves for the journey to the east, but when they eventually gathered at Venice in the summer of 1202 as agreed, there was a major problem. The cost of the venture had been based around the figure of 33,500 fighting men turning up, but only 11,000 men had appeared. That meant the crusaders still owed Venice 34,000 silver marks – despite their searching of pockets and wringing of hands the Venetians remained firm. Not only was it embarrassing for the debtors but, crucially, it gave Venice the leverage with which to direct the course of the crusade.

To move the situation forward, Enrico Dandolo made a suggestion to the crusaders: if they helped the Venetians retake the port of Zara, across the Adriatic on the Dalmatian coast, which had recently been captured by the Hungarians, then Venice would consider a postponement of their debt. Many crusaders immediately objected to the idea of an attack on a Christian town, especially since the king of Hungary had himself just taken the cross (his possessions, therefore, were supposed to be under church protection). When Innocent got wind of the plan, he expressly forbade such an assault. But to the majority of the crusaders, the prospect of their grand expedition fizzling out around the sleepy lagoons of Venice was too much to bear, and they agreed to the plan. So in the late autumn of 1202, the combined forces of Venice and the crusaders, led by the doge in his vermilion-painted galley, set out for Zara, arriving on November 10. The port was soon taken and the Venetians and crusaders proceeded to squabble over the spoils like vultures over a carcass. Innocent himself was incandescent and excommunicated the entire attacking force, although he later lifted the ban on the crusaders.

BYZANTINE POLITICS

The crusaders' and Venetians' next move was now determined by a proposal made by Philip of Swabia, the king of Germany, which involved the labyrinth that was Byzantine politics. Philip had married the daughter of the Byzantine emperor Isaac II Angelus, an elderly, ineffectual ruler who in 1195 had been deposed by his brother, thrown into prison and blinded. Isaac's son, Alexius, had also been imprisoned but had then managed to escape and make his way west to the court of his brother-in-law, Philip. There, it seems, Alexius hatched the plan that Philip's envoys now presented to the crusaders, who were wintering in Zara. In return for their help in getting rid of his usurping uncle (Alexius III) and placing him on the throne, the young Alexius would pay off the crusaders' debt to Venice and bankroll their expedition to Egypt, to which he would add a 10,000-strong Byzantine force. He would also pay for the maintenance of 500 Byzantine knights in the Holy Land for the rest of his life and make the Orthodox Church submit to the authority of Rome.

The proposal had some obvious advantages, not least slicing through the Gordian knot of the crusaders' financial problems. But not all approved of the idea of disobeying the pope and interfering in the affairs of Christendom's greatest city, and a number of crusaders made their way east under their own steam. The majority, however, were delighted at the opportunity now presented to them. The proposal of Philip and Alexius was duly accepted – Pope Innocent's formal protest at the new plan was to arrive too late – and at the end of April 1203, the fleet sailed from Zara for Constantinople. Proceeding by way of Corfu, where they were joined by Alexius, and the southern tip of the Peloponnese, the armada headed across the Aegean to the island of Andros and thence to the Dardanelles. On June 24 the fleet dropped anchor opposite Constantinople. According to Geoffrey of Villehardouin, one of the crusade's chroniclers, the westerners were amazed to see the sheer size and grandeur of the city, with its countless ramparts, towers, palaces and churches – even the doughtiest warriors shivered at the sight of such a marvellous metropolis. Although forewarned of the crusaders' advance, the usurping emperor, Alexius III, had made no great preparations for the defence of the city. Equally, Prince Alexius's assurances to the westerners that he would be greeted with open arms by the common people did not materialize.

ABOVE *The 5th-century walls of Constantinople were a formidable obstacle to besiegers. The crusaders finally gained access to the city via the less imposing fortifications facing the Golden Horn.*

CONSTANTINOPLE IN CONFLICT

In early July the crusaders attacked Galata on the other side of the Golden Horn from the main city and broke the huge iron defensive chain that was strung across the inlet to prevent ships penetrating it. They then sailed their ships up the Horn, ready to mount an assault on the walls. On July 17, led with great courage by Enrico Dandolo himself, the Venetians stormed the walls near the palace of Blachernae in the north-west of the city and put the terrified defenders to flight. Meanwhile, that evening, Alexius, the usurper, decided that he had had enough of imperial responsibilities and quietly slipped away from the capital. Bereft of their emperor, the Byzantines extricated their blind old emperor Isaac Angelus from prison and set him back on the throne. They then sent a message to the westerners saying that since Prince Alexius's father was now back in power there was no justification for continuing the assault. The Venetians and crusaders, however, insisted that Alexius should be made co-emperor with his father and that the bargain Alexius had made with them should be honoured. The Byzantines were in too parlous a position to quibble, and on August 1, 1203, Isaac was joined by his new co-ruler, Alexius IV, his son.

Now that he was in power, Alexius had to address the promises he had made to the crusaders, and his chickens soon came home to roost. The imperial treasury lacked the funds to reimburse the Venetians, and the taxes Alexius imposed to raise money were resented. The Orthodox clergy were aggrieved at his attempts to make them acknowledge papal supremacy, and furious when he ordered church silver to be melted down to boost the money supply. As Alexius tried to appease the crusaders, who were anxious to sail on to Egypt, the latter grew angry and impatient at the delay. The people of Constantinople became infuriated with their emperor for what they saw as his cringing obeisance toward the westerners, whom they despised as uncouth, lecherous thugs, committing acts of vandalism, such as burning down a mosque used by visiting Muslims – the blaze had spread and reduced a quarter of the city to ash.

As tensions rose in January 1204, the citizens of Constantinople, led by a noble named Alexius Murzuphlus, rose in revolt and deposed both the young Alexius IV, who was strangled, and his father Isaac, who died shortly afterward, probably murdered. Brutal though the actions were, at least now the Byzantines had a leader who would be patriotic, decisive and aggressive. As Murzuphlus set labourers to work on building up the walls, the crusaders, too poor to venture to the east or head back home, were no longer in any doubt as to what action they should now take. Enrico Dandolo had been setting before their eyes the tempting advantages of capturing Constantinople and placing one of their own on the Byzantine throne, and now Murzuphlus's challenge to their military strength was forcing their hand.

Before mounting an assault, however, the westerners thought it prudent to sort out first who should reign as emperor once the city was taken – it did not seem to occur to them that they might fail in this regard. Boniface of Montferrat, the overall leader of the crusaders, was the obvious choice, but the Venetians objected to him on account of his associations with their trading rivals, the Genoese. So it was decided to appoint a committee of 12, comprising six Franks and six Venetians, who would elect an emperor after the city's fall. If the new emperor turned out to be a Frank, then, it was agreed, the patriarch should be a Venetian, and vice versa. Other arrangements were also made, for example about the apportionment of captured territory and loot.

ABOVE *The Golden Horn is the great inlet of water that bisects Constantinople. It was protected from enemy shipping by a huge metal chain strung across its entrance.*

COSTATINO POLIM

THE SACK OF CONSTANTINOPLE

With the post-victory decisions sorted out before their assault, the crusaders began their first attack on April 9, 1204. The Venetian warships and galleys moved up the Golden Horn in formation and in some places came so close to the walls that sailors high up in the ships' towers could joust with the Byzantine defenders. Yet despite sustained assaults at a number of different points the crusaders were beaten back. On April 12, the crusaders tried again; this time they were counterattacked by Byzantine ships, which were unable to stop the westerners' advance. As a north wind drove the crusaders' ships, some of them tied together, toward the walls, one or two knights leapt onto the ramparts directly from the ships, while soldiers jumped off the transport vessels, pushed scaling ladders up against the walls and swarmed upward to overwhelm the defenders. Once an initial breech had been made the siege was effectively over. There were too few defenders, and the loyalty of those who did fight had been undermined by the quick turnover of emperors.

After victory had been secured, the westerners' leaders allowed their troops to go on the rampage for three days, the usual allotment for successful besiegers. In one of the most destructive

sacks ever known, the people of Constantinople were murdered, raped and robbed. Priceless, centuries-old treasures were looted or destroyed. The Byzantine chronicler Nicetas Choniates described how the frenzied westerners smashed sacred icons and tore jewels out of chalices, which they used as drinking cups. They poured into the great church of Hagia Sophia and broke up the high altar into pieces, which they distributed among themselves. Horses and mules were brought into the church to help carry off the silver and gold ripped from the pulpit, throne, doors and furniture. They placed in the chair of the patriarch a prostitute, who sang bawdy songs and danced provocatively. Outside, screams and cries filled the air.

Those crusaders whose minds were not totally befuddled by a lust for violence paused long enough to appropriate souvenirs rather than destroy them. The Venetians, for example, took the four bronze horses that had stood in the city's hippodrome since the days of its eponymous founder, Emperor Constantine I, and transferred them to Venice, where they stood proudly outside the basilica of St Mark. In one of the city's churches, a Cistercian monk named Martin made a Greek priest show him, on pain of death, the hiding place where the sacred relics were kept. The monk took away a haul that included the arms, feet and teeth of various saints along with a splinter of the True Cross.

After the prescribed three days of bloody mayhem, the crusaders settled down to organize the government of the city and its territories and to apportion the spoils. The council of Venetians and crusaders ended up electing a Frenchman named Baldwin of Flanders and Hainault as emperor – he was crowned on May 16, 1204 – and the Venetian Tommaso Morosini as patriarch. The Venetians, as had been agreed, were given three-eighths of the city and various parts of Romania – as the new Latin empire of Constantinople was called – that would best serve their maritime trading operations, as well as the right to trade freely throughout the empire. Elsewhere, Frankish nobles installed themselves in various parts of Greece and other European regions of the empire. Boniface of Montferrat presided over Thessalonica; Otto de la Roche governed Boeotia and Attica; and the Peloponnese was controlled by William of Champflitte, who was shortly succeeded by Geoffrey of Villehardouin, a nephew of the crusade's chronicler. These new western rulers made little attempt to win the hearts and minds of the Greek populace, on whom they tried to impose the Latin liturgy whenever they could.

Meanwhile, in the west, the news of the fall of Constantinople and the influx of sacred treasures was greeted with delight and the singing of hymns. At first Pope Innocent, despite his original reservations about the expedition, was extremely pleased with the way events had turned out. But after he received more and more gory details of the pillaging he changed his mind and condemned the outrages. But his heartfelt protestations were too late. The sack of Constantinople, which was to accelerate the city's decline until it was finally captured by the Turks in 1453, lodged itself in Greek consciousness for centuries to come. Even in 2001, Pope John Paul II, during a flying visit to Athens, saw fit to issue an apology for what had happened in April 1204.

Although the Byzantines had been expelled from their capital, they still retained strong footholds in a few places within the empire, for example at Trebizond on the south-eastern shore of the Black Sea, and especially at Nicaea, where Theodore Lascaris, the son-in-law of Alexius III (the usurper), was proclaimed emperor in 1206. It was from Nicaea that the Greeks would eventually regain Constantinople 57 years after its loss. In 1258 a Greek nobleman named Michael Palaeologus came to power in Nicaea, and his forces decisively defeated a Frankish army in western Greece in 1259. Then on June 25, 1261, some Nicaean troops, probing Constantinople's defences, found the city undefended and promptly captured it: it was not long before Michael was crowned emperor in Hagia Sophia amid joyful celebrations.

ABOVE *Venice was founded on water and thrived on maritime trade.*

VENICE: THE MOST SERENE REPUBLIC

By the time of the Fourth Crusade, Venice – known as *La Serenissima*, the Most Serene Republic – was one of the largest cities in Europe, with a population of about 70,000 people. Its leadership and success during the crusade ensured that it would be the dominant power in the eastern Mediterranean during the first half of the thirteenth century. Bitter enmity between Venice and Constantinople was manifested in the crusade, with Venice plundering many Byzantine treasures, but the two sides had actually been close allies for much of the republic's history.

Situated on small islands north of the Po estuary in north-eastern Italy, Venice came into being in the sixth century AD, after the arrival of Roman refugees fleeing the incursions of barbarian invaders. As the city grew it managed to maintain a balance of interests between the west and the Byzantine Empire, whose cultural traditions it absorbed. By a treaty concluded in 810 between Charlemagne, emperor of the west, and Nicephorus, the Byzantine emperor, Venice was acknowledged as being within the Byzantines' sphere of influence but was also given trading rights in Carolingian lands. In the late 820s the city's identity solidified when, according to legend, two Venetian traders arrived back home from Alexandria in Egypt bearing, in a pork barrel, what they claimed were the bones of St Mark, apparently pilfered from his burial place. To house the sacred relics the basilica of St Mark was constructed (later completely rebuilt in the Byzantine style in the eleventh century), and the saint's symbol, the lion, became that of the republic.

Venice grew as a commercial power during the tenth century, as it exerted control over the Adriatic Sea. In 992 the Byzantines granted the city trading privileges, including a reduction in customs dues, as a reward for giving them military aid. The association between Constantinople and Venice was further strengthened in about 1082 when Venice supplied ships to the empire in its fight against the Normans in Byzantine-held southern Italy. In return, Emperor Alexius Comnenus allowed the Venetians the right to trade duty-free throughout most of the empire and to set up warehouses and other facilities in Byzantine ports.

During the twelfth century, Venice consolidated its wealth and power, which was firmly based on its government-backed merchant fleets and its vibrant shipbuilding industry – by 1150 about 16,000 workers were employed in its state-owned shipyards. During the same century, however, Venice fell out with its Byzantine allies. Part of the problem lay in the fact that the Byzantines had grown to resent the Venetian community in Constantinople, whom they considered to be too rich and arrogant. At the same time, the Venetians were angered by the Byzantines granting trade concessions to their Italian rivals, Genoa, Pisa and Amalfi. Then, in 1171, a serious assault against the Genoese who had recently settled in Constantinople's district of Galata gave Emperor Manuel Comnenus the excuse to act against Venice. He blamed the Venetians – even though the perpetrators were never identified – and decreed that all Venetians living in the Byzantine Empire should be arrested and have their property confiscated. The republic reacted by sending out a war fleet of 120 vessels to attack Constantinople, but a combination of Byzantine delaying tactics and plague ensured it never reached the Bosphorus. Thirty years later, however, the Venetians under Enrico Dandolo took full revenge.

toute le feu dont dieu
le gart a petit pont.
Or difons dont q̃
quant grace nous
fift dieu le tout puiffãt
quant il nous deffen

Ci devife comment da
miete fu prinfe.

di de mort et de peril a la
riuer la ou nous arriua
mes a pie et courumes
fus a nos ennemis q
qui eftoient a cheual.

rant grace
nous fift
noftre feig
neur de da

miete que il nous de
liura. La quele nous
ne deuffions pas auoir
prife fanz affamer. Et

6

ON THE BANKS OF THE NILE

The Fourth Crusade had been a disaster for Christendom. Constantinople had been ravaged and the Byzantine Empire dismembered, its long-term prospects for survival weakened. The reputation of the Franks had been irrevocably blackened in the eyes of the Greeks, and the Christians of the Latin east, hoping for reinforcements and support from the west, had not received any substantial assistance. Pope Innocent III also fully appreciated the lasting damage that had been done to his hopes of a reunion between the Latin and Greek churches. Nevertheless, despite his eventual outrage at the crusade's bloody denouement, Innocent still maintained his enthusiasm for a great expedition to the east.

THE LOST CHILDREN

I ndeed, the spirit of crusading seemed to be more ubiquitous than ever in the early thirteenth century. Apart from the situation in Palestine, there were opportunities to fight pagans in the Baltic or Muslims in Spain, where a great Christian victory at the battle of Las Navas de Tolosa in 1212 re-ignited the *Reconquista*. For French knights, in particular, there was the possibility of killing the heretical Albigenses in Languedoc. The heady crusading atmosphere of the time is perhaps best captured by the strange and tragic episode of the Children's Crusade, which has a folkloric, pied-piper resonance to it. The crusade involved what appears to have been a spontaneous gathering of children both in France and Germany, who were inspired by the thought that where the strong and powerful had failed to recover the Holy Land, the poor and lowly might succeed, in accordance with Christ's teachings that the "meek" might "inherit the earth".

The leader of the French children was a 12-year-old boy named Stephen, who in May 1212 travelled with some companions from his village near Chartres to the court of King Philip Augustus at Saint-Denis. Stephen carried a letter that he claimed had come from Christ himself, bidding Stephen to preach a new crusade. Although the king found the boy and his epistle less than convincing, Stephen felt he had found his life's vocation. He began to travel around France, exhorting children to join him on a great expedition to the east, promising them that the sea would part before them – just as it had done for Moses and the Israelites when fleeing from Egypt to the Promised Land of Canaan – and they would be able to walk dry-shod to Palestine. The many youngsters who were eager to follow his lead gathered at Vendôme in late June, as Stephen had commanded, and from there they set out south for Marseilles. Contemporary chroniclers, always prone to exaggerating numbers, claim there were up to 30,000 children and their hangers-on marching down the byways of France. Led by Stephen in his horse-drawn cart, the children proceeded by way of Tours and Lyons; but soon heat, hunger and thirst took their toll, killing some and persuading others to return home.

ABOVE *The Children's Crusade, here depicted by the 19th-century French artist Gustave Doré, saw thousands of children march from northern France to Marseilles – and disaster.*

The children's morale improved when they finally reached Marseilles and the sympathetic concern of its citizens. But then the unthinkable happened: the sea refused to part before them, and many became instantly disillusioned with Stephen and left. Those who stayed loyal to him, hoping that the miracle might yet happen, were then approached, it is said, by two local merchants whose actions and names, Hugh Ferreus and William Porcus (Hugh Iron and William Pig), were those of pantomime villains. The two men offered to transport the children to the Holy Land free of charge, and the young crusaders, perhaps believing that God worked miracles in more than one way, gladly accepted the offer. Nothing more was heard of them for 18 years. Then in 1230 a survivor of the expedition, a young priest, returned to France from Egypt and related what had happened. The party had set out from Marseilles in seven ships, but two of them had been wrecked off the coast of Sardinia. The remaining five vessels had then been captured by Muslim pirates, who had apparently been tipped off by Hugh and William. The children were taken to Algeria, where some were sold into slavery, while others met the same fate after a journey to the markets of Alexandria. The priest himself had been enslaved but was later released.

The German children's crusade fared little better. Shortly after Stephen had been rousing his peers in France, a German boy named Nicholas followed suit in the Rhineland, where he urged the local children to leave their homes and follow him to Palestine in order to convert the Muslims. As was the case with Stephen, Nicholas's words were like yeast in the imaginations of the youngsters who heard him, and within a few weeks thousands of children had gathered at Cologne, ready for the great expedition to the east. The Germans proceeded in two groups. The first, led by Nicholas, marched via the Swiss Alps to northern Italy, a gruelling trek that many of the young pilgrims did not survive.

Those who reached the port of Genoa in August 1212 received a kindly welcome; but, as at Marseilles, the sea stubbornly declined to part, and disillusionment set in, with many children accepting the Genoese offer of becoming citizens. Nicholas, however, was not beaten yet. He took his deflated but game companions to Pisa in the hope that the sea might yet perform a miracle. When again that did not happen, he led his band to Rome, where he obtained an audience with Pope Innocent. The latter was respectful of their devotion and courage but firmly insisted that they should return to their homes. His words ended their march; but few made it back to the Rhineland – what exactly happened to the majority is shrouded in mystery. Nicholas himself, it seems, never returned, and the anger of the bereft Rhineland parents was visited on the boy's father, who was killed by a lynch mob.

The expedition of the second party of German children also ended in pathos. They, too, had to cross the Alps before walking to Ancona in north-eastern Italy. When the sea proved as recalcitrant in the Adriatic as it was in the Mediterranean, the children marched south along the coast to Brindisi, where the crusade fizzled out. Some managed to find ships to take them to the Holy Land, while others cut their losses and straggled home – few are known to have made it back.

A PAPAL RALLYING CRY

The whole phenomenon of the Children's Crusade seems like a subconscious parody of the great knightly expeditions that had been mounted up to that point; yet it did nothing to deter or alter the crusading spirit among Europe's adults. At the Fourth Lateran Council of 1215, Pope Innocent again made an appeal for a crusade to the Holy Land, setting the departure date as June 1, 1217, the time when a truce made between the Muslims and Franks was due to expire. In the spring of 1216, preachers fanned out across Europe to persuade people to take the cross and were sometimes assisted, it is said, by miraculous visions. In the Low Countries a great cross bearing the form of a human body was seen, while elsewhere in the region a white cross moved slowly through the sky as if pointing the way to Jerusalem. But the Fifth Crusade, which was now

coming into being, was not to be witnessed by its principal architect, Innocent, who died of an illness in the summer of 1216. His place was taken by Honorius III, a pope whose enthusiasm for the crusading ideal matched that of his predecessor.

The fruits of the papal preaching operation had, in fact, limited results. The French nobles, who usually could be relied upon to fill out the higher ranks of any crusading army, were largely preoccupied with the Albigensian Crusade, which was raging in southern France at this time. But there was a better response from Austria and Hungary, where respectively Duke Leopold VI (the son of the Duke Leopold who had imprisoned Richard the Lionheart) and King Andrew II raised armies and prepared for the journey. In September 1217, both men set sail from the Adriatic port of Split – however, the bulk of the crusader force had to follow on several months later since the vessels provided by Venice were too few.

Soon after Leopold and Andrew arrived in the Holy Land they were joined by King Hugh of Cyprus and his small army. Although the three commanders had relatively few troops at their disposal – probably in the region of 5,000 men – they were welcomed at Acre by the current king of Jerusalem, an elderly man named John of Brienne. He held the crown by virtue of his marriage to Maria, the kingdom's young hereditary queen. John realized the dangers of keeping sizeable contingents of soldiers unoccupied and suggested a spot of campaigning in Palestine. Agreeable to this idea, the commanders led their forces out in November 1217, but a combination of ill discipline and bad cooperation among the troops ensured that very little was achieved. The small town of Beisan, south-west of the Sea of Galilee, was taken, and this was followed by a rather desultory march around Galilee then west back to Acre. In December, John himself launched a small, solo expedition against a Muslim stronghold on Mount Tabor, south-east of Nazareth, but he failed to capture it and had to retreat back to Acre again.

THE EGYPTIAN PRIZE

After a few months of under-achievement, the Hungarian king, Andrew, decided he had had enough of Outremer life and in January 1218 headed back home overland through Anatolia, having obtained a promise from the Seljuk sultan that he would be allowed to pass safely. Duke Leopold elected to stay, but he and King John took no further offensive action until the arrival of a Frisian fleet in April 1218 bringing reinforcements. With more troops at their disposal, the commanders discussed plans, and the consensus was that an attack should be made on Egypt – supposedly the Muslims' soft underbelly and the original objective of the Fourth Crusade. (After Saladin's death, his empire had been split among members of his Ayubid family, with the ruler of Egypt generally regarded as the senior figure in the region. However, the Ayubids were usually too busy fighting among themselves to concentrate on the Franks.) The gist of the Christians' thinking was that if they took Jerusalem without having first secured Egypt then a counterattacking Muslim pincer movement from Egypt and Syria would be hard to resist. But if they took Egypt, the Muslims' richest region, then Jerusalem would be at their mercy. So Egypt it was, with the port of Damietta on the Nile Delta the first major target.

RIGHT *The Nile and its delta, shown in this satellite photograph, provided the battleground for the opposing armies of the Fifth Crusade. The town of Damietta lay two miles upriver from the coast and was protected by a huge chain strung across the Nile.*

ιρκῶρ. Ηραῖοδὲκαιγώσοκάαχῶππῶολοῦππυρι·

ι̂ ῶ τ̂
μου πυρπολ ΤΟΗΤΩΝΕΗΛΗΤΙΦΟΛΟΝ·

ABOVE *Greek fire, shown being used in a naval battle in this Byzantine illumination, is often referred to as "medieval napalm". Consisting of an explosive cocktail of sulphur and resins, it was effectively employed by the Muslim defenders of the chain tower just north of Damietta.*

On May 24, 1218, a Christian fleet under the command of King John left Acre and headed for the ancient land of the pharaohs. By the end of the month, the crusaders were camped on the west bank of the Nile, about two miles downstream from Damietta, ready for the first engagement. One of the principal components of the town's northern defences was a huge chain stretched across the Nile from its east bank to a strongly garrisoned tower standing on an islet near the west bank. Like the chain across the Golden Horn in Constantinople, Damietta's effectively blocked the progress of any river traffic, so it was imperative for the Franks to capture the tower. The first attempts to storm it failed. But then a German named Oliver of Paderborn, who became a chronicler of the crusade, devised and had built a sea-borne siege tower, which was constructed on two ships roped together and armoured with metal sheets and animal hides to protect it from enemy fire. On August 24, the crusaders launched this floating tower and guided it close enough to the Muslim fort for a drawbridge to be dropped down on it, allowing assault troops to run across and secure a position. Despite fierce fighting by the cornered Muslim garrison, the crusaders prevailed, and were soon able to dismantle the chain across the Nile.

For the Muslims, the loss of the tower was a disaster, since the fall of Damietta now seemed inevitable. The news appears to have hastened the elderly and sick sultan, al-Adil, the brother of Saladin, to his grave. But in fact Damietta did not fall at this time. If the crusaders had made an immediate attack on the town, capitalizing on their momentum, they might have succeeded, and Egypt would have fallen like a ripe plum into their laps. Instead they dug in, preferring to wait for the reinforcements that Pope Honorius was expected to be sending, and settled down to a conventional siege. The pope's army duly arrived in September 1218 and was led by a Spanish cardinal named Pelagius, a zealous, authoritarian and rather insensitive individual, who lacked military experience and managed to exacerbate the barely dormant rivalries that existed between the crusaders' various commanders. A second contingent of Christian troops, from France and England, arrived in October, swelling the attackers' ranks but resulting in no further positive action. In November a fierce storm and floods wrecked the Christian camp, and this was followed by an outbreak of plague, which killed a sixth of the army and left the survivors drained, physically and mentally.

DEADLOCK ✠ AT DAMIETTA

By February 1219 morale among the Christians was so low that Pelagius decided an assault against the Muslim relief army, under al-Adil's son al-Kamil, which was camped nearby, was paramount, if only to keep the troops occupied. After their initial advance had to be aborted owing to a rainstorm, the Christians learned that al-Kamil had made a sudden, panicky retreat because he had learned of conspirators in his midst, ready to murder him. The crusaders saw their chance, pushed forward and managed to reach a position south of Damietta, thereby enveloping the town. In turn, having rooted out the scheming traitors in his inner circle, al-Kamil, now reinforced by the army of his brother al-Mu'azzam, tried to regain the ground he had lost through his precipitate withdrawal, but his attacks against the Christian positions foundered. Damietta was at the mercy of the crusaders: the Muslim relief force could make no headway and the town's garrison was decimated by plague.

The crusaders were sure enough of their position to turn down an offer made by al-Kamil, that in return for their evacuation of Egypt he would cede Jerusalem and the central parts of Galilee and Palestine and ratify a 30-year truce between the two sides. Yet they were still too unsure of their strength to make a decisive assault on Damietta. Eventually, as the Egyptian summer began to inflict its burning heat, and disease took its toll on the crusaders, Pelagius decided to increase the pressure on Damietta with a series of bombardments and assaults, all of which achieved nothing but a further dip in the attackers' morale. At this point, some crusaders, following the lead of Duke Leopold, who had left Egypt in May, now returned home, leaving Pelagius and King John to wrangle over the leadership of the army and points of strategy.

It was at this time of scorching heat and frustration that Francis of Assisi, the founder of the Franciscan order of friars (see Box, p. 89), made a charming cameo appearance amid the crusade's blood and thunder. Wishing to achieve by the word of God what the crusaders were trying to obtain

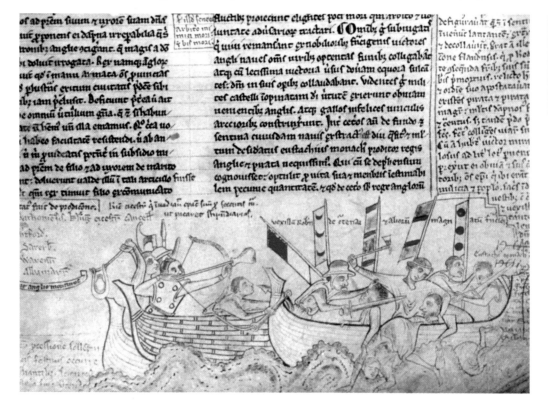

LEFT *Armed with swords, axes and bows, Christians and Muslims engage in hand-to-hand combat in a naval battle on the Nile during the siege of Damietta.*

ABOVE *St Francis of Assisi preaches to a languid Sultan al-Kamil in this 19th-century French woodcut. The friar failed to convert the sultan, who treated his visitor with great respect.*

FRANCIS OF ASSISI: THE SAINTS' SAINT

The meeting between Francis of Assisi and Sultan al-Kamil is one of the most intriguing encounters of the crusading period. It pits one of Islam's most powerful leaders against one of the most attractive figures in the history of Christianity – the man who, through his love of humanity and nature and his profound humility, was widely held to be the saints' saint. In fact Francis had planned missions to the Muslims in Syria and Morocco on two previous occasions, but the expeditions had to be abandoned because of shipwreck and illness. Although his attempt to convert al-Kamil failed, he set an example for future Franciscan friars, whose missionary endeavours would eventually reach the Far East and the New World.

The son of a rich cloth merchant, Francis was born in the town of Assisi in Umbria in 1182. At first, as a typical young man of his time, Francis spent his days enjoying the pleasures of life. But his destiny changed radically while he was journeying to the south of Italy to pursue a career as a soldier. In a dream a divine voice told him to return to Assisi – it was one of a number of supernatural signs that pointed him toward a spiritual way of life. Others included the time when he was praying before a crucifix in a church near Assisi and heard God tell him to "go and repair my house because it is falling into ruin". Francis took the words literally and sold some of his father's merchandise to raise money for the church. After this, despite the angry protest of his father, he renounced his inheritance and embraced a life of absolute poverty.

The seal on Francis's spiritual conversion occurred in 1208 when, while attending Mass, he heard a gospel reading in which Christ urges his disciples to go out into the world and preach the gospel and heal the sick, adopting a life of absolute material poverty. The words struck Francis like a bolt of lightning, compelling him to take action; and he was soon joined in his dedication to holy living and good works by a small group of followers – who became the nucleus of the Franciscan friars, or Friars Minor, as they were formally called.

Innocent III, the great crusading pope, formally approved the new movement in 1210, and in the following year Francis and his companions embarked on their mission to bring the word of God to the most underprivileged members of society. They slept rough and begged for their food (hence the Franciscans were a "mendicant" or "begging" order) and, through their evident piety, they attracted large numbers of recruits. One of them was an Assisi woman named Clare, after whom Francis founded the Poor Clares, an order for women who wished to pursue Franciscan ideals.

After several years of working in Italy, Francis was filled with the urge to take Christ's message abroad – an impulse that led to his trip to Egypt in 1219. When he eventually returned to Italy, he had to tackle various problems concerning his friars, who had grown enormously in number. Basically, the movement, as it became more unwieldy, was finding it difficult to maintain its commitment to Francis's original ideals of simplicity and poverty. And although he was universally admired for his saintliness and charisma, Francis was not a great organizer. So, recognizing that it would benefit the order if someone else took over the supervision of its practical affairs, Francis stood down as its leader at an assembly of about 5,000 friars in 1221.

During his last years Francis continued his life dedicated to Christ's gospel, and in 1224 he received a vision that consummated his spiritual yearnings. While praying on Mount La Verna in the Apennines, he saw a six-winged seraph in the form of the crucified Christ. After the vision had gone Francis found that he bore the stigmata, the five marks of Christ's wounds, on his hands and feet and the right side of his body. By this time, however, Francis's health, undermined by incessant toil, ascetic living and illness, was beginning to fail. He lived on for another two years, but eventually died near Assisi on October 3, 1226, at the age of 44. He was proclaimed a saint by the pope two years later.

ABOVE *The humanity of St. Francis is emphasized in this fresco by the 13th-century Florentine painter Cimabue.*

by the sword, Francis had sailed to Egypt and made his way to the Christian camp. His objective was nothing less than to talk Sultan al-Kamil, nephew of the great Saladin himself, into becoming a Christian. Having obtained Pelagius's permission to make this solo expedition, Francis made his way a few miles south to the Muslim camp at Fariskur under a flag of truce. Disarmed by *Il Poverello*'s humble, if not dishevelled, appearance and obvious charisma, the Muslim guards led him to al-Kamil. The sultan politely listened to what Francis had to say but was not inclined to change his faith. Instead, in recompense, he tried to press expensive gifts onto his visitor – which Francis politely declined to accept – then had him escorted back to the Christian camp.

A HOLLOW VICTORY

By September 1219, with still no end in sight to the stalemate between the two sides, al-Kamil decided again to press for a truce, his hand being forced by the failure of the Nile flood that year and the resulting desperate shortage of food. The sultan offered the same terms as before but with the attractive addition of the relic of the True Cross, captured by Saladin at the battle of Hattin. Many of the crusaders were inclined to accept it, King John among them. But Pelagius had his principles, and one of them was refusing to come to terms with the infidel. In addition, the commanders of the military orders pointed out that unless the Muslim fortresses east of the River Jordan were also handed over then Jerusalem could never be successfully defended against future Muslim counterattacks. But al-Kamil would not countenance the loss of his Transjordan strongholds, since they ensured the viability of the vital supply line between Egypt and Muslim Syria. So in the end Pelagius and his supporters prevailed, and the offer was turned down.

Shortly afterward, it seemed that Pelagius's firm stance had been vindicated. The crusaders discovered that the walls of Damietta were practically undefended and made a sudden sortie on November 5. They virtually walked into the town unopposed, since the garrison and townsfolk had been struck down by an epidemic. The fall of Damietta was a crucial, if ultimately unheroic, victory for the crusaders, and it raised heady hopes that the whole of Egypt – indeed, the Muslim Middle East – might tumble like a house of cards. Such aspirations, however, soon gave way to mundane reality. A quarrel broke out between Pelagius and King John as to who should govern the town. Then resentment and discontent over the spoils spread to other parts of the army. By February 1220, King John had had his fill of squabbling with the papal legate and sailed home to Acre, where he soon had to counter the threat of a Muslim invasion of his kingdom.

For the next ten months the crusaders remained in Damietta, making themselves at home but achieving very little else. But the prospect of positive action became more realistic when, at the end of 1220, Pope Honorius sent a message saying that the Holy Roman Emperor, Frederick II, was preparing to sail out east in the spring of 1221. In fact Frederick did not embark at this time – although he was to influence dramatically the affairs of the Latin kingdom at a later date – but he did send Louis, duke of Bavaria, with a powerful force. Indeed, it was the prospect of the arrival of Louis that made Pelagius again turn down another offer of peace – comprising more or less the same terms as before – made by al-Kamil in June. It was a decision he would later regret.

DEFEAT ON THE NILE

Soon after Louis arrived in Egypt, the crusaders decided to march southward before the annual rising of the Nile made such an advance impossible. King John was persuaded to join the new expedition – not without reluctance – and on July 17, 1221, the Christian host headed south down the east bank of the Nile, leaving a contingent to guard Damietta. A few days later the Christians had occupied the town of Sharamsah, while the Muslim army waited for them in a strong position about 20 miles (32 km) upriver at Mansurah. Then, on July 24, against the advice of King John, the Christians set up camp in a position bounded by the Nile and one of its tributaries. But as the Nile waters rose, the Muslims crucially managed to move troops by land and by canal behind the crusaders, cutting off their retreat back to Damietta. Suddenly, the Christian commanders realized they were encircled, with enough rations for only three more weeks. Their only hope lay in a prompt withdrawal.

On August 26 the Christians struck camp and headed north; but the Muslims, spotting fires from the camp stores which the crusaders had unwisely torched, became aware of the evacuation and acted quickly. With the Nile continuing to rise, they opened several river sluices so that water poured over the fields that lay in front of the retreating crusaders. Bogged down in muddy, swampy terrain, and harassed by Muslim cavalry and foot-soldiers, the Christian army was on the brink of a disaster. Stalwart work by King John and the military orders managed to fend off several Muslim attacks. But by the end of August Pelagius realized he had to sue for peace, with the hope that his only strong bargaining chip, the city of Damietta, might carry some weight. Sultan al-Kamil knew the strength of his negotiating position but did not press his advantage too far. For the surrender of Damietta and an eight years' truce he would let the Christians withdraw from Egypt and also give back the True Cross (which in the end could not be found). This time Pelagius had no choice but to agree – and doubtless he reflected ruefully on the missed opportunities of acquiring Jerusalem. On September 8, 1221, the crusaders sailed away from Egypt, thereby bringing the Fifth Crusade to an ignominious close.

LEFT *The Nile's annual flood proved to be a major stumbling block for the Christian army of the Fifth Crusade. The river's waters created the swampy, unmanageable terrain on which the Christians foundered and were forced to seek terms with the enemy.*

difficilia cape
bimus artis.
niquenq̄
ex sola sua
deueniem o
pito ipm lee
nimq̄ bndc
cum ars ha
pria q̄ adm
7 nos non i
dra. l. nato
omibz
nidebancu
illega postic
bimu. li

7

JERUSALEM REGAINED

The Fifth Crusade had involved a long bloody conflict and the tantalizing, but lost, opportunity to regain Jerusalem from Muslim control, but the crusade of the Holy Roman Emperor Frederick II Hohenstaufen, from 1228 to 1229, was exactly the opposite. The emperor negotiated the return of the holy city into Christian hands and a ten-year truce between the Latin kingdom and the Muslims in a relatively short period of time and without spilling a drop of blood. It was a remarkable feat, especially considering Frederick had a relatively small force at his disposal and had carried out his crusade while under the ban of excommunication, rendering him an outlaw of the church and a pariah in the eyes of many of the Frankish barons. Indeed, Frederick's expedition was one of the most peculiar episodes in the history of the crusades, and one that somehow typifies the character and style of its architect. He was a man of brilliance and imagination, of cruelty and ruthlessness, who seemed to dazzle his contemporaries, some of whom referred to him as Stupor Mundi, the Wonder of the World.

FREDERICK II: "WONDER OF THE WORLD"

ABOVE *Frederick (1194–1250), shown at left, is crowned emperor in this illustration from a French psalter.*

One of the most fascinating characters of the thirteenth century, Frederick II was known to his contemporaries as *Stupor Mundi*, Wonder of the World, and many stories, some probably apocryphal, describe him and his exploits with awe. A well-built man of middling height, he had the red hair of his German forebears, green eyes and sensual lips. He was a gifted linguist and could speak German, Italian, French, Greek, Latin and Arabic fluently; he wrote poetry in the Sicilian vernacular and authored a book on the art of falconry. Blessed with an intellectual curiosity (he was, appropriately, the founder of the University of Naples), he enjoyed studying philosophy, medicine, geography, natural history and science. A story about two men who had dined at his table suggests that he was a pioneer of the empirical method. He ordered one to go to bed immediately and the other to go off hunting; later on, he had them both disembowelled to see which one had digested his food the better.

Frederick's attitude to religion in an age when piety was taken seriously, if only in appearance, was unusual and complex. It is said that he joked about God being ignorant in granting such a barren land as Palestine to the Jews; and that he once declared that Moses, Jesus and Muhammad had deceived the world. Yet it seems that he believed God had granted him his kingly status, he had a genuine interest in theology and religious practices, and he was conventionally pious. He studied Islam and did not believe that the Orthodox Church should be branded schismatic for not accepting the authority of Rome. Not only Christians of different traditions but also Muslims and Jews were allowed to practise their faiths openly in his Sicilian kingdom. Yet his relatively liberal or sceptical religious views never hampered his political instincts. He savagely persecuted Christian heretics when it suited him, and he had no hesitation in uprooting and transporting his Muslim citizens in Sicily to the Italian mainland for fear that their proximity to their co-religionists in northern Africa might prove to be a threat to his kingdom.

His morals and habits were also unusual for the time. He maintained a harem, supervised by eunuchs, in Sicily, where his various wives were kept. And when he travelled he took with him an entourage that included a Muslim bodyguard, jesters and executioners, along with his treasures and menagerie. The latter included an array of exotic animals, such as bears, lions, leopards, ostriches and even an elephant and a giraffe. His colourful, autocratic nature was, in short, more typical of an eastern despot than the Holy Roman Emperor, the supposed guardian of the church.

After Frederick's return to Italy from Palestine, he quickly defeated the papal army that had been raised against him, and Pope Gregory IX was forced to lift his excommunication of the emperor by the terms of the treaty of San Germano in 1230. But Frederick's domestic problems were to continue. In the following years his patched-up relationship with Gregory broke down again, and this was followed by a fierce propaganda offensive by the pope. In Germany, misrule by his son, Henry, resulted in a revolt by the nobles and Frederick having to depose Henry in 1235. When Innocent IV came to the papal throne in 1243 in succession to Gregory, the antagonism between pope and emperor intensified, with anti-imperialists branding Frederick as the antichrist. In 1245, because of the imperial threat, Innocent was forced to flee from Rome to Lyons, where he held a synod at which he excommunicated Frederick and called for him to be deposed. For the last five years of his life, Frederick was constantly at war, fighting battles in Italy. He was gaining the upper hand in the north of the country when he fell ill in 1250 and died. He was buried in Palermo in Sicily.

A COSMOPOLITAN CHAMPION

Crusading was in Frederick's genes. His grandfather was Frederick I Barbarossa, one of the leaders of the Third Crusade, who had drowned in an Anatolian river en route to Palestine; and his father was Emperor Henry VI, who had organized an expedition to the Holy Land but had died in 1197 before sailing there himself. Henry had married Constance of Sicily, who was of royal Norman blood, and on his death the three-year-old Frederick inherited the kingdom of Sicily (which included large parts of southern Italy). Even though he was half-German and half-

Norman, Frederick thought of himself as an Italian, and he revelled in the exotic, cosmopolitan atmosphere of his kingdom, where Byzantine, Muslim and Norman intellectual and cultural traditions were mixed together.

Frederick's status as western emperor, combined with his great wealth, made him the perfect Christian champion to take the fight to the infidel – someone who could restore the crusading movement's prestige after the disastrous Fourth and Fifth Crusades. Yet, although he had taken the cross as early as 1215, Frederick had for various reasons delayed setting out to the Holy Land, much to the frustration of the papacy.

But in 1225 a new hope was kindled in Pope Honorius that Frederick would at last honour his crusading vows. It was announced that the emperor, a widower for three years, would marry Isabella II (also known as Yolande), the 14-year-old daughter of John of Brienne and heiress to the throne of Jerusalem. Surely now, it was thought, Frederick would take steps to restore Jerusalem as the capital of what would shortly be his new kingdom by virtue of his forthcoming marriage. The wedding duly took place in Brindisi on November 9, and immediately afterward Frederick showed the darker side of his nature. It is said that having humiliated his father-in-law over his claim to be regent of Jerusalem, the emperor proceeded to seduce one of his new wife's cousins during the honeymoon. He then packed Isabella off to his oriental-style harem in Palermo in Sicily.

THE EMPEROR DELAYS

To placate the pope, Frederick had sworn before his wedding that he would definitely set out for the Holy Land – but not quite yet: the summer of 1227 was the best he could promise, and the pope had to settle for that. In the interval the emperor concentrated on trying to establish his rule in northern Italy. Papal-imperial relations changed, however, when Honorius died and was succeeded by Gregory IX, a more dynamic and inflexible pontiff whose belief in the supremacy of the papacy matched Frederick's idealized conception of being emperor. The two leading figures of Christendom were set on a collision course.

As the departure date of the crusade loomed closer, Frederick made the appropriate preparations, and this time it seemed he really would be on his way to the east. In August 1227 an advance contingent of imperial troops under Henry IV, duke of Limburg, set sail from Brindisi, and in early September Frederick himself boarded a ship for the Holy Land. Yet just after his departure, as fate would have it, one of his nobles fell seriously ill and Frederick decided to put in at Otranto on the heel of Italy. There, the noble died, and Frederick himself fell ill. Having sent off the rest of the fleet eastward, he then retired to Italy to convalesce. For Pope Gregory, however, this was all too much to bear. He was singularly unimpressed by what he construed to be another outbreak of imperial procrastination and trickery. Taking drastic action, he immediately excommunicated Frederick for breaking his vows, and solemnly repeated the excommunication a few months later in St Peter's, Rome. This time Frederick had a genuine excuse for his delay, and with great indignation issued a rebuttal

ABOVE *Pope Gregory IX faces monks and other churchmen in this 13th-century French illumination.*

RIGHT *A seated Pope Innocent IV declares Emperor Frederick an outlaw of the church to attentive bishops at the council of Lyons. This illustration is taken from the Chronicles of the 13th-century Englishman Matthew Paris.*

of the pope's accusations to Europe's princes. He then proved the earnestness of his intentions by preparing to sail in the summer of 1228.

By this time, however, Frederick's position as a crusader had changed radically in two ways. Now, as an excommunicate, he was not legally permitted, according to church law, to go on a crusade. Not only that, his wife Isabella had died just after giving birth to their son Conrad in April 1228, which meant that Frederick was no longer the king of Jerusalem by virtue of his marriage, but only regent for his son, who was now the rightful heir to the throne. With Pope Gregory unable to stop him, the emperor left Brindisi on June 28, 1228, and set sail for the east – this time there were no impediments to prevent his journey. At the end of August he and his party arrived at Cyprus, where he tried to pressure the acting governor, John of Ibelin, the leading Outremer baron, into handing over some of the island's revenues. John stood his ground and eventually a compromise was reached – but it gave the barons of the Latin kingdom a foretaste of the emperor's personal authoritarian style.

Frederick set out from Cyprus on September 3 and arrived at Acre four days later. His reception was mixed. There was a degree of enthusiasm among the common people, but the nobles had strong reservations. They were used to rulers who saw themselves as first among equals, not autocrats. Frederick was different. He had a much more ancient and oriental, that is more exalted, conception of kingship: he saw himself as the divinely appointed servant of God with absolute powers. Rubbing shoulders with, and taking advice from, the local nobles was not part of his style. Also, there was the problem of his excommunication. The clergy, led by the patriarch, Gerold, and the orders of the Hospitallers and Templars, who were obedient to the pope, had no wish to associate with someone under papal ban. The Teutonic Knights, however, were prepared to support Frederick, if only because their master was an old friend of his.

Bereft of the armies of the two main military orders, Frederick had a problem with manpower, being able to rely on only about 10,000 troops in total – hardly a host to furrow the brows of the

Muslims. He therefore realized that his best hope of success lay in diplomacy; and it was part of the positive side of his character that he should consider negotiations an acceptable way of dealing with the enemy, unlike most of his predecessors, for whom glory through bloodshed was paramount.

BLUFF AND COUNTER-BLUFF

I t was fortunate for Frederick that his chief Muslim adversary was Sultan al-Kamil of Egypt, who, as was apparent in the Fifth Crusade, was ever ready to countenance peace plans with his Christian opponents. In addition, since the last crusade, the Muslims of the Middle East had been embroiled in domestic squabbles, ending any possibility of them facing the new crusade with a united front. Their problems were based around the jealousies and rivalries of al-Kamil and his two brothers, al-Mu'azzam, who governed Syria, and al-Ashraf, who controlled the area of what is now northern Iraq. Indeed, to counter what he perceived to be the potential threat of his brother al-Mu'azzam, al-Kamil had actually sent one of his trusted emirs, Fakhr ad-Din, to Frederick in 1226 to ask for military aid. The emperor had received the emir warmly (and later actually knighted him as a mark of their friendship) and listened to al-Kamil's proposals, but had kept his options open. A year later, however, the political situation among the Muslims changed, and al-Kamil had cause to regret his request for help from Frederick. What happened was that al-Mu'azzam died on November 11, 1227, which meant that Damascus and its territories was now in the hands of his callow young son, an-Nasir. It did not take long for the boy's two uncles to size up the new opportunities presented to them. Agreeing to parcel up Syria between them, al-Kamil and al-Ashraf advanced with their armies and toward the end of 1228 laid siege to Damascus, where an-Nasir had taken refuge.

Naturally, al-Kamil, who no longer needed Frederick's help, was dismayed when he learned that the emperor had actually arrived on Palestinian soil, since it meant that with a Christian army at his back he could not wholeheartedly commit himself to besieging Damascus. It was true that his initial overtures to Frederick had been met with a friendly response; but al-Kamil fundamentally trusted Frederick as little as Frederick trusted him. So he again sent out his emissary Fakhr ad-Din to the emperor at Acre to discuss the possibility of a truce. Instructed to spin out the negotiations for as long as possible, Fakhr ad-Din engaged Frederick in congenial discussions for several months, during which time the orientalized emperor and his westernized Muslim opponent enjoyed the thrust and counter-thrust of political haggling, with each of them anxious to score a diplomatic victory. Al-Kamil needed a resolution to enable him to concentrate on his siege of Damascus, while Frederick, having heard disquieting news that Pope Gregory was raising an army to invade his kingdom of Sicily, knew he could not stay long in the Latin kingdom.

By the end of November 1228, with the bluffs and counter-bluffs between him and al-Kamil wearing thin, Frederick decided that a spot of military posturing – a march to Jaffa, where he ordered his troops to build up the defences – might increase the pressure on his opponent. But the sultan was not unduly bothered by what he saw correctly as a bargaining ploy, and the poker game continued. In the end, however, it was al-Kamil who was the first to capitulate. By February 1229 he had still failed to capture Damascus and he was now ready to make an offer he hoped Frederick would accept. In return for peace and the emperor's departure, he would cede Jerusalem, along with a corridor connecting it to the coast, as well as Bethlehem, Nazareth and various territories in Galilee and around Sidon. However, in Jerusalem itself, the Muslims would keep hold of their holy places, the Dome of the Rock and the al-Aqsa mosque on Temple Mount, and they would be permitted access there and the right to worship freely. There would also be an exchange of prisoners-of-war and a ten-year truce.

A HOLLOW VICTORY

Frederick accepted the terms, and once again Jerusalem, without any blood being shed, was back in Christian hands. An excommunicated emperor, a personal enemy of the pope and a religious sceptic had succeeded where many others, filled with religious zeal and martial fire, and supported by huge armies, had noticeably fallen short. It was a personal triumph for Frederick. But if he had imagined that church bells would be ringing out in celebration he would have been disappointed. To the pope he was still a detested enemy. The Frankish nobles were not happy with him either. They realized that the new borders were strategically precarious – one of the reasons that Cardinal Pelagius had turned down more or less the same peace terms during the Fifth Crusade. They were also uneasy about Frederick's designs on the kingship of Jerusalem, since after all he was still only regent for his son, Conrad. Also, the more zealous Christians were furious that the Muslims had been left with places of worship in the holy city, and many, including the Templars, Hospitallers and the patriarch, were still unrelenting in their attitude toward the emperor's excommunication. For his part, al-Kamil fared even worse than Frederick: in the eyes of ordinary Muslims he was a traitor to his faith. And an-Nasir, besieged in Damascus, pointedly ordered his citizens to go into public mourning for what Islam had lost to the Christians.

Despite his fellow Christians' grumblings and resentment, Frederick received the keys of Jerusalem on Saturday March 17, 1229, and marched into the city with his personal guard and the Teutonic Knights. There was no cheering in the streets, because they were empty. The Muslims had evacuated the city and the native Christians waited sullenly behind closed doors, fearing that life under the new Latin Christian rule might be worse than that under the sultan. On Sunday morning Frederick went to the priest-less Church of the Holy Sepulchre, utterly disregarding his sentence of excommunication, and there he placed on his own head the crown of Jerusalem. He then withdrew to discuss plans for fortifying the city. Later, he decided to make a tour of the city's Islamic shrines and was puzzled when he failed to hear the traditional Muslim call to prayer. When he learned that it had been suppressed out of regard for his finer feelings he was indignant and declared that one of the reasons he had come to Jerusalem was to hear it. His sensitivity toward Islam was also shown when he set foot on Temple Mount to view the Dome of the Rock and the al-Aqsa mosque. He spotted a Christian priest following in his wake and immediately had him thrown out, giving strict orders that any Christian trespassers should be put to death.

Yet despite Frederick's evident curiosity at the Dome of the Rock, his use of Arabic slang and quick-witted responses to his guides, the Muslims did not warm to him. They were intrigued by this multilingual, philosophy-discussing Frank, who clearly wielded great power; but they could not help noticing that he was disrespectful to his own faith, and this made him suspicious in their eyes. They could understand, and perhaps even respect, the likes of a Cardinal Pelagius, intolerant and arrogant, but at least burning with religious zeal. But Frederick seemed to revel in agnosticism. He was neither fish nor fowl: how could they trust him?

The next day, Monday, the patriarch Gerold's representative arrived to place Jerusalem under an interdict (a prohibition of religious services) for receiving the excommunicated emperor. At this Frederick's patience snapped and he left the city forthwith, arriving in Acre four days later. There, he was met by angry Frankish barons, resentful of the way he had concluded the deal with al-Kamil without their agreement. During the month of April, Frederick tried to settle his affairs in Palestine before returning home, resisting the strong urge to use force to neutralize his Christian enemies, including the Templars. Disturbing news then reached him from Italy: a papal army under John of Brienne, his father-in-law, had invaded his realm. Without delay, he appointed two governors to look after the kingdom of Jerusalem, then prepared to sail on May 1 – in the early hours of the morning so as to escape the hostile attention of the townsfolk. But as his company proceeded through Acre down Butchers' Street, he was pelted with offal and muck and verbally abused – so much so that two local nobles had to restore order. These two men then escorted Frederick to his ship and bade him a polite farewell; the emperor could see there was no love lost between them and cursed the men openly. He then set sail from Acre and journeyed via Cyprus to Brindisi, arriving there on June 10, 1229.

Frederick's main crusading achievement, the return of Jerusalem, was considerable, especially given the difficult circumstances in which he was operating. But to a great extent he created his own problems, for example in his attitude toward the local nobles. His autocratic view of government was at odds with the loose-knit, decentralized model the Frankish barons had adopted through force of necessity. And his disregard for his sentence of excommunication alienated the two main military orders, whose support he could not easily afford to lose. In effect he had no choice but to negotiate rather than to fight, and he was fortunate that al-Kamil's position was ultimately weaker than his own. Although he left Palestine with Jerusalem in Christian hands, the city still bore an air of insecurity, for everyone knew that the Muslims could retake it at any time. The rancour that he stirred up among the barons continued well after his departure. Instead of celebrating the return of the Holy City and the peace made with the Muslims, they warred among themselves.

OPPOSITE *Louis IX, king of France, later canonized as a saint, sets out on his first crusade in this 14th-century book illustration. Louis's two expeditions, to Egypt and Tunis, both ended in failure.*

THE SAINT'S PROGRESS

The years following Frederick II's diplomatic crusade in the Holy Land were marked by political chaos and infighting not only among the Franks of the Latin east but, fortunately for them, among their Muslim opponents as well. Following the end of the truce between Frederick and al-Kamil in 1239 there came two relatively low-key crusades under Count Thibald IV of Champagne (1239-40) and Richard of Cornwall (1240-41). These were notable less for pitched battles than for negotiated truces, which succeeded in slightly enlarging the Latin kingdom's boundaries. The general lack of stability at this time led to fluid politics and expediency, with Christians and Muslims ready to form alliances with each other if necessary. This was the case in 1244, when war broke out between the Muslim rulers of Egypt and Damascus. The Franks actively supported the Damascenes, a decision that was to prove costly. The Egyptians formed an alliance with the Khwarazmian Turks, bellicose tribesmen who had been driven from their heartland in central Asia to the region of Mesopotamia by the even more ferocious Mongols. At the suggestion of the Egyptian sultan, the Khwarazmians invaded Syria to attack Muslims and Christians alike.

In June 1244, about 10,000 Khwarazmian horsemen galloped southward, burning and pillaging as they went. The walls of Damascus rebuffed them, so they swept onward into Galilee then south to Jerusalem itself. The Holy City put up little resistance, and the Turkish warriors had a free hand in destroying and looting. Churches were torched, priests murdered, and the venerable bones of Jerusalem's kings were removed from their tombs and scattered. Jerusalem was to remain in Muslim hands until the 20th century – the next Christian army to enter the city would do so in 1917, when the British commander General Allenby captured it from the Ottoman Turks during World War I.

Galvanized by this new threat to their security, the Franks immediately prepared to make a counterattack. On October 17, 1244, in conjunction with their Damascene and other Muslim allies, the Christians advanced to confront the Egyptians and Khwarazmians at the village of La Forbie, near Gaza. The battle was hard fought, but in the end the Franks and their allies were outmanoeuvred and finally destroyed. It was a disaster for the Franks, who could ill afford the loss of manpower. Only the continued struggle between Damascus and Egypt saved the Latin kingdom from total perdition.

ST LOUIS, THE MODEL CHRISTIAN KING

Described by a medieval chronicler as having "an angelic countenance and a gracious person", Louis IX, king of France, became renowned for his spiritual nature and austere private life, his sense of justice and generosity, and he was widely held to be the embodiment of the ideal Christian ruler. The king's piety was unusually sincere for a Christian potentate – he is said to have remarked that "there is no leprosy so foul as being in mortal sin", and he heard Mass twice a day. He was also an inveterate supporter of the crusading movement and an avid collector of holy relics – he built the magnificent Sainte-Chapelle in Paris to house the Crown of Thorns, which he had bought from Baldwin II, the Latin emperor of Constantinople, in 1239. Yet his profound feeling for religion and respect for the church did not deter him from standing up to the papacy when he needed to. When Pope Innocent IV, during his struggle with Frederick II, tried to impose taxes on France to raise money for his cause, Louis would not hear of it.

Louis was born in Poissy in 1214, the eldest son of King Louis VIII and Blanche of Castile. After his father died in 1226, Louis was crowned king at the age of 12, although his redoubtable mother acted as regent – indeed, she would later govern France when her son was absent crusading in the east. In 1234 Louis married Margaret of Provence, a high-spirited woman who accompanied him to Egypt on his first crusade and would bear him 11 children. Although Louis's first crusade ended in disaster on the banks of the Nile, by the time he returned to France, after skilfully managing the government of the Latin east for a few years, his reputation as a crusader was, if anything, stronger. Although he spent more time

outside France than his mother would have wished, Louis did initiate important administrative reforms regarding the country's system of law and its national finances.

Yet it is perhaps for his personal character that Louis is best remembered. Throughout his life, he set high standards of morality. He was scrupulously honest toward friend and foe alike. After his capture by the Egyptians in 1250, one of his French nobles told him that he had cheated the Muslims out of 10,000 pounds of the required ransom money and Louis was furious, ordering the money to be paid. He also had a passion for justice: before setting out on his first crusade in 1247 he established a commission of *enquêteurs* or investigators to inquire into complaints made by the people against royal administrators. Yet he was by no means a soft, liberal monarch. His rule was absolute, and he could be as harsh as anyone in certain matters, especially religion. Blasphemers were severely punished (for example by having their lips and noses burnt) and heretics hunted down – Louis was an active supporter of the Inquisition, which resulted in many being burned at the stake in Burgundy, Champagne and elsewhere. And his religious zeal led him to take a malign view of the Jews.

Louis's reputation for being fair and just became so great that he was considered to be a more able arbitrator of disputes than the pope. This included disputes outside his realm, such as in the Low Countries, and even in England, where he arbitrated between King Henry III and his barons. Above all, he desired peace and justice with other nations, united under a common faith.

ABOVE *This painting by the 16th-century Italian artist Berto di Giovanni conveys Louis's piety as well as his majesty.*

It was against this background that Louis IX, king of France, a ruler whose piety, integrity and sense of justice were outstanding by the standards of the times – he was later canonized by Pope Boniface VIII in 1297 – made the first of his two crusades against the Muslims. The fall of Jerusalem coupled with his recovery from a serious illness in December 1244 – he had vowed to take the cross if he survived it – pushed Louis into making preparations for a great expedition to the east. The king spent the next three years raising money and putting his affairs in order. At last, in August 1248, Louis and the cream of French chivalry, along with a small number of knights from other parts of Europe, including a contingent of English crusaders under William, Earl of Salisbury, set sail for Cyprus, arriving there in mid-September. Once all the commanders had gathered on the island, they discussed plans and decided to attack Egypt, which they, like the leaders of the Fifth Crusade, considered to be the chink in Islam's armour.

RETURN TO DAMIETTA

Wintering in Cyprus, Louis finally set sail for Egypt in the spring of 1249 and arrived off the Egyptian coastline by Damietta on June 4. The sultan of Egypt, as-Salih Ayub, who was elderly and sick, made hasty preparations to counter this latest Christian expedition. He revictualled and garrisoned Damietta and sent a force under his vizier Fakhr ad-Din – the man who had negotiated with Frederick II some years before – to fight Louis as he disembarked.

Despite the threat of a large Egyptian force, and ignoring advice to wait for the rest of his fleet to arrive, Louis decided to land at daybreak on June 5. As the sun rose, the French knights stormed ashore and quickly dug their shields and lances into the sand to form an impenetrable wall of steel against the imminent Egyptian attack. According to John of Joinville, one of the crusade's chroniclers, the king himself, in impetuous mood, leapt into the sea from his ship and waded through the chest-high water, holding his sword aloft and bearing his shield around his neck. When he reached dry land and saw the Egyptians ranged before him he had to be physically restrained from charging at them there and then.

Instead it was the Muslims who attacked first. But failing to make any headway against the disciplined crusaders, the Egyptians were eventually compelled to retreat, and Fakhr ad-Din led them back over a bridge of boats across the Nile to Damietta. There he found the citizens and garrison in such a state of bewildered terror that he decided to move out straightaway. Seeing the army leaving them, the Damiettans were thrown into greater panic and fled in pursuit. First, they set fire to their storehouses of provisions but, crucially, not the bridge of boats, which facilitated the Christian advance. When Louis and his men learned of the Muslim evacuation there was great rejoicing and singing of the hymn *"Te Deum Laudamus"*. Whereas the knights of the Fifth Crusade had taken nearly a year and a half to capture Damietta at great cost of life, the French now walked into an empty city just after arriving in Egypt.

The crusaders, however, were unable to capitalize on their stunning triumph. Louis had sensibly done his homework and knew it would have been futile to advance while the Nile was still in flood. Instead he decided to consolidate his position in Damietta and wait for reinforcements from France. The Christians set about converting the main mosque into a cathedral and apportioning buildings and areas of the city to the military orders and the Italian maritime states of Pisa, Genoa and Venice. As the weeks passed, however, the crusaders' initial buoyancy was dissipated by morale-sapping inaction, food shortages and the sweltering Egyptian summer, which brought disease. But nothing could be done until the autumn and the recession of the Nile waters.

The Muslims, meanwhile, were mortified by the loss of Damietta, and the ailing Sultan Ayub tried to negotiate its return by offering Jerusalem in its stead. But Louis, like Cardinal Pelagius on the Fifth Crusade, would not do business with infidels on principle. Would he, like Pelagius, have cause to regret turning the offer down?

THE MARCH SOUTH

By the end of October 1249, the Nile waters had receded and the French reinforcements had arrived. With renewed optimism, Louis decided that the next objective would be Cairo, more than 100 miles (170 km) to the south. On November 20 he marched his men out of Damietta toward Mansurah, where, three days later, Sultan Ayub died. His passing away might have thrown Egypt into crisis but for the quick action of his widow, Shajar ad-Durr, who concealed her husband's death for long enough to make critical court and government appointments, including that of Fakhr ad-Din as commander-in-chief, thereby stabilizing the ship of state.

The Christians' march south was slow and guarded, hampered by innumerable canals and riverlets that intersected the road, as well as by Egyptian cavalry raids. Finally, in December, the Franks reached the broad canal known as the Bahr as-Saghir, which cut across them just before Mansurah and behind which Fakhr ad-Din had drawn up his forces. For the next few weeks crusaders and Muslims faced each other across the canal. The Christians attempted to build a dyke across the water as a bridge, but the ferocious onslaught of stones and Greek fire, the brilliant, burning light of which turned night into day, made progress painfully slow. So slow, in fact, that when an Egyptian peasant volunteered, for the sum of 500 bezants, to lead the crusaders to a ford where they could cross the canal they accepted the offer at once.

At daybreak on February 8, 1250, the bulk of the crusading army, with contingents of French, led by Robert of Artois (Louis's brother), Templars and English in the vanguard, slowly began crossing the water by the ford. Once on the other side, Robert, instead of waiting for the rest of the army to arrive as the king had instructed, decided to mount an attack immediately on the Egyptians, camped a couple of miles outside Mansurah. With about 1,500 knights he swept into the enemy positions, catching them completely by surprise. The crusaders rampaged around, cutting down their half-dressed, half-asleep opponents. Fakhr ad-Din, who had finished his morning bath and was completing his toilette, heard the shouts. Straightaway, without donning his armour, he jumped onto his horse, galloped into the mêlée and was promptly dispatched by a troop of knights. With the scent of victory and glory in his nostrils, Robert then decided, against the advice of the Templars and English, who urged him to wait for Louis, to forge ahead and take Mansurah itself. The decision turned out to be disastrous. As the crusaders charged headlong

Opposite Clad in golden armour and encircled by a halo, Louis IX arrives at Damietta in Egypt in this late medieval illumination. In fact Louis and his men occupied the city, which had been abandoned by the Muslims, without a fight.

through the open gates they found themselves in a lethal labyrinth of tiny streets. With the knights hemmed in on all fronts, their horses rearing up as Muslim soldiers attacked them from all angles, it was more like shooting fish in a barrel than a battle. Virtually everyone was killed, with Robert of Artois and William of Salisbury among the fallen.

When Louis heard of the catastrophe he immediately prepared his troops, who had now crossed the Bahr as-Saghir, for an Egyptian counterattack, which was not long in coming. All day long the battle ebbed and flowed, until finally the Muslims beat a retreat back to Mansurah. Louis had had the last say, but he was distraught over the loss of his brother Robert. Three days later the Egyptians again tried to drive the Christians back into the canal, and again Louis held firm. Something of a stalemate now ensued. As days turned into weeks, the pressure on the crusaders' manpower and resources increased, especially after the Egyptians transported boats overland and launched them behind the crusaders' lines to intercept their supply vessels. Then the inevitable hunger, dysentery and typhoid began to bite.

DISASTER ON THE NILE

By April 1250 Louis knew he had no alternative but to retreat as best he could to Damietta – a scenario horribly familiar from the events of the Fifth Crusade. The king's belated attempts to negotiate with the new sultan, Turanshah, failed; so on April 5 the gruelling trek down-river began, with the king courageously taking his place in the rearguard, which was most vulnerable to Muslim attacks. Indeed, the Egyptians were quick to spot the retreat and began their harassment straightaway. They were only just fought off by the sick and exhausted crusaders. On April 6, Louis, stricken with illness, could hardly stay on his horse, and the rest of his army began to crumple before the onslaught of the full weight of the Egyptian army. Surrender was the only option, with the hope that Damietta – still in Christian hands and being ably governed by Louis's wife, Queen Margaret – could be used at the bargaining table. The Muslims took the king and his leading nobles back to Mansurah, but, unable to cope with the huge haul of Christian prisoners, they butchered many of the wounded and those not worth ransoming.

In prison, Louis was the exemplar of dignity and bravery, impressing friend and foe alike. But he had no choice but to agree to Egyptian terms: a huge ransom of 800,000 bezants and the cession of Damietta in return for his and his army's lives. Yet no sooner had this offer been made than it was jeopardized by a change of regime in Egypt. On May 2 Turanshah had suddenly been murdered by members of the

RIGHT *Amid mayhem and dismembered bodies, King Louis, shown right of centre on horseback wearing a crown, is led away captive during the retreat to Damietta in this illustration from the medieval* Life and Miracles of St Louis.

Mamluks, the sultan's elite army corps, led by a man named Baybars, who in later years would become the scourge of the Franks. The Mamluks themselves were white slaves brought mainly from the central Asian steppes to the courts of Muslim rulers, where they were converted to Islam. They were then trained in the arts of war and were especially feared as mounted archers. The death of Turanshah saw the rise to power of the Mamluks – their dynasty would last some two hundred years until the time of the Ottoman Turks.

Shortly after Turanshah's assassination, the Mamluks, only after some heavy-handed threats to their Christian captives, decided to ratify the original treaty, insisting that Louis pay half the ransom in Damietta and half after he had arrived in Acre. The king agreed and with some (enforced) financial help from the Templars he managed to pay the first instalment before setting sail to Acre on May 6. And so the crusade ended. It had been an unmitigated disaster. Even so, Louis decided that instead of washing his hands of the whole episode and returning home he should stay and try to make amends for his failure. Also, he was ever mindful that there were still Christian prisoners in Egypt waiting to be freed. As the senior Christian figure in Palestine, and with the titular king of Jerusalem, Conrad – Frederick II's son – still absent, Louis became in effect the ruler of the Latin east, a state of affairs welcomed by the Frankish barons.

ABOVE Mamluk cavalry perform military exercises in this 14th-century Egyptian illumination. The Mamluks were renowned for their bravery, discipline and horsemanship.

THE LAMB AND THE CROSS

News of Louis's defeat and capture by the Egyptians was received with shock back in Europe, particularly by his own people. One result of this was what was called the "crusade of the shepherds", a phenomenon not unlike the Children's Crusade. Like the latter, the shepherds' crusade involved the spontaneous mobilizing of the poor and lowly in society, except that this time they consisted of shepherds and labourers rather than children. Their leader was an enigmatic, 60-year-old figure known as the "Master of Hungary", whose powerful sermons, long beard and saintly demeanour attracted thousands to his cause. He began preaching at Easter 1251, when he declared that the poor and simple could achieve in the Holy Land what their feudal superiors had failed to do. Carrying banners emblazoned with the lamb and the cross, representing humility and victory, and armed with swords and axes, the shepherds marched to Paris, where the Master was interviewed by Louis's mother and regent, Queen Blanche. The queen, at first, gave encouragement to this strange man's mission. But the shepherds, whose discipline was fragile and temperament anti-clerical, began to run riot, killing priests and damaging churches. Then after a rally of the shepherds at Orléans turned to violence, the queen soon decided to suppress the crusade.

While his mother was coping with affairs in France, Louis was trying to supervise the Latin kingdom as best he could. Although short of manpower, he was fortunate that the Muslims were in no position to capitalize on the Christian defeat at Mansurah. The brutal murder of Turanshah, who was Saladin's grandson, was shocking to supporters of the Ayubid dynasty, and hostilities broke out between Damascus and Mamluk Egypt. When the moment seemed propitious, Louis threatened the Mamluks with a Frankish alliance with Damascus and persuaded them to forego the

GENGHIS KHAN AND THE MONGOLS

One of the great military leaders of all time, the Mongol ruler Genghis Khan built up an empire on the steppes of Asia and China that was so vast it was said it would take two years to traverse it by foot. He accomplished this through ruthlessness, brilliant organization and force of personality. Genghis could be cruel – one defeated foe had his eyes and ears filled with molten silver; yet he promoted religious tolerance in his territories and established a rule that was just and fair to everyone.

Temuchin, the man who was to become Genghis Khan ("Universal Emperor"), was born in 1162 in Siberia and grew up into a tall, tough, determined and charismatic young man. He soon became renowned for

were hardy and courageous, and so well trained that they could change formation at great speed and skilfully execute tactics such as the feigned retreat – luring the enemy into an ambush. Genghis also used terrorism and propaganda effectively: cities that dared to challenge his authority were mercilessly destroyed and their inhabitants massacred as a dire warning to others.

Imbued with a spirit of conquest, Genghis led his troops on foreign expeditions and it was not long before northern China felt the might of his army. The Great Wall held up the Mongol advance for a while; but in 1215 Genghis subjugated the Chin Empire, taking its capital Peking (Beijing) and driving the emperor to the south. In 1219 Genghis turned his attention to the west. His army overran the empire of the Khwarazmian Turks, capturing the great cities of Bokhara and Samarkand in 1220. When Genghis died seven years later, his empire stretched from the Pacific Ocean in the east to the Black Sea in the west.

The death of Genghis did nothing to halt Mongol expansion. His son Ogodai, who became Great Khan in 1229, savagely suppressed revolts by the Chinese and the Khwarazmian Turks, and in 1237 his forces swept into southern Russia, eventually reaching Poland and other parts of eastern Europe. Throughout the rest of the century the Mongols continued their campaigns of conquest so that by 1300 they were in control of China, Iran and

ABOVE *Genghis Khan holds court in oriental splendour in this medieval Persian illumination.*

his military prowess and, by 1206, he had united various Mongol and Turkic tribes by force or diplomacy into a potent military force and become their ruler. His next step was to reorganize the army. He imposed a regime of strict discipline on his troops and arranged them in units of tens, hundreds, and thousands. Mongol forces moved and fought on small, swift ponies, and their main weapon was a powerful bow, which could hit an opponent up to 200 yards (180 metres) away. Genghis's men

huge areas of Anatolia and Russia. But the empire that had expanded so spectacularly was destined to wither relatively quickly. It had been beset and weakened by internal divisions and rivalries for some time before the last great Mongol leader Timur Lang (Timur the Lame) or Tamerlane came to power in the latter half of the fourteenth century. From his capital of Samarkand, Timur retook Iran in 1379 and invaded and ravaged northern India. In 1402 he defeated the Ottoman Turks at Ankara, thereby delaying the latter's assault on Constantinople. But on Timur's death in 1405 his empire was broken up by his sons, and the Mongols disappeared as a world power.

rest of the outstanding ransom money and to release their Christian prisoners, which they did in March 1252. Louis also tried to strengthen Outremer's position by enlisting allies. He signed a treaty with the Assassins, and even sent ambassadors to the Mongols – who, under Genghis Khan and his successors, had become the most formidable military power in the world – with a request for assistance against the Muslims in Syria. Then, in April 1254, with problems in France demanding his attention, Louis decided that it was time to go home. In the aftermath of his failed crusade he had done much to stabilize the Latin kingdom, a tribute to his political skills, tact and the immense esteem in which he was held by Christians and Muslims alike.

THE GREAT KHAN

Just before Louis set sail for France, one of his ambassadors to the Mongols, William of Rubruck, arrived at their capital of Karakorum in Mongolia and was granted an audience with the Great Khan, Mongka. William was not the only emissary seeking the help or friendship of the Mongols: representatives of the Muslim caliph of Baghdad, the Seljuk sultan and assorted emirs were there, as were ambassadors from the Byzantine emperor and various Russian princes and the king of Delhi. For by this time the Mongol Empire was the largest in the world and the reputation of its huge, disciplined and ferocious army was so high that few rulers could afford not to explore diplomatic channels with the Great Khan. But William of Rubruck found discussing the possibility of an alliance between the Franks of the Latin east and the Mongols difficult. Hopes had been raised by the fact that Mongka was well disposed toward Christianity because his beloved mother had been a Nestorian Christian. The problem, however, was that the khan, in the words of Sir Steven Runciman, "could not admit the existence of any sovereign prince in the world other than himself. His foreign policy was fundamentally simple. His friends were already his vassals; his enemies were to be eliminated or reduced to vassaldom." Such uncompromising, if courteous, megalomania gave William little succour: Mongol aid would be forthcoming so long as the king of France paid homage to the khan – terms no king of France would accept. William wended his way back west through central Asia and over the Caucasus and eventually reached Acre – empty-handed.

Yet there was one Christian ruler who did make a deal with Mongka. This was Hethoum, the king of Armenia, who had been quick to perceive the potential threat of the Mongols and wished to harness their power in order to destroy his Muslim enemies. Willing to submit himself as a Mongol vassal, Hethoum spoke to Mongka soon after William had left, and the khan agreed to return Jerusalem to the Christians if they gave support to his brother Hülegü in his planned attack against the Muslims of Mesopotamia and Syria. When Hethoum returned home, bearing this proposal, the common people were enthusiastic; so was Bohemond of Antioch, who happened to be Hethoum's son-in-law. But the other Frankish barons of Outremer were extremely wary of the Mongols and did not want to commit themselves.

THE MONGOL ONSLAUGHT

In January 1256, Hülegü began the Mongol advance, leading a vast force across the River Oxus. With typical Mongol thoroughness, engineers travelled in front, making good the roads and bridges; siege-machines were transported all the way from China; and herds were led away from their pasturelands so that Hülegü's horses would have sufficient food. The Mongols' first objective was the Assassins' headquarters of Alamut in Iran, which was destroyed. After virtually the entire sect had been exterminated in the region during the course of 1257, Hülegü moved on to his next goal, Baghdad, the capital of the Abbasid caliphs and of Sunni Islam. The current caliph, al-Mustasim, commanded a huge army, but his court was undermined by internal feuding. Nevertheless, Hülegü was not entirely sanguine about the forthcoming confrontation.

On January 11, 1258, the caliph's army encountered a Mongol force about 30 miles (50 km) west of Baghdad and, when it retreated, followed it in pursuit – into a trap. Having lured their opponents onto swampy ground, the Mongols proceeded to dismantle dykes on the Euphrates in order to flood the fields behind the Arabs. Forced back by the Mongol army into a quagmire, the Muslims were thrown into chaos and destroyed. But Baghdad, with its formidable fortifications, had still to be taken. By January 22 Hülegü had surrounded the city and was bombarding the eastern walls; al-Mustasim could see the end coming and sent ambassadors to make terms with Hülegü, who refused to see them. On February 10 the Mongols poured through the smashed walls and began their trademark massacre. For days the slaughter continued – no one was spared except for a few children who were sold into slavery and the Christian population, who had been given immunity and were found cowering in their churches. An estimated 80,000 people were killed, and the stench of the dead and the likelihood of disease drove Hülegü and his men from the city. The fall of Baghdad was a major landmark in the history of Islam, for it spelled the end of the centuries-old Abbasid caliphate and left a power vacuum at the heart of Islam.

cecons de mansul et parlerons de laudas la grant cite.

De la nobleste de la cite de baudas et de lestat 7 du siege du calif. Baudas est vne cite la ou estoit le calife de tous les sarrazins du monde. ainsi conme est a rome le siege du pape des crestiens. et parmi la cite auoit vn moult grant flun. Et parmi cestun puet on aler en la mer dinde qui abien .xviii. iournees de baudas. Si que moult grant quantite de marcheans y vont et viennent auec leur marchandise. et arriuent en vne cite qui a nom cisi. et dillec entrent en la mer dinde. Encore sur le flun entre baudas...

RIGHT *The Mongol commander Hülegü orders the caliph of Baghdad to reveal to him the city's treasury in this 15th-century French illumination. After Hülegü had got what he wanted he put the caliph to death.*

RIGHT *The Mongols besiege Baghdad in February 1258 in this Persian book illustration. After the city's fall the Mongols murdered thousands of men, women and children with their trademark savagery.*

Hülegü's next target was Syria, and his advance seemed to be irresistible. In January 1260 Aleppo fell – again the Muslims were massacred and the Christians spared – then Christian Antioch paid the Mongol leader homage, much to the disgust of the other Franks, who now saw the Mongols as a greater threat than the Muslims. Indeed, the Franks of Acre sent a letter to Charles of Anjou, King Louis's brother and a powerful, influential figure in Mediterranean politics, asking him for help against the Mongols. No aid was to come, and in March Hülegü captured Damascus – apart from the citadel, which later fell in April. With Damascus, Baghdad and Aleppo, three great jewels of Islam, in Mongol hands, it looked as if the whole of the Muslim Middle East would collapse: only the Mamluk regime in Egypt, under Saif al-Din Qutuz, who had become sultan in December 1259, stood in the khan's way.

THE SAINT'S PROGRESS

THE MUSLIM REPLY

But events following the death of the Great Khan, Mongka, in August 1259 helped to save Islam. With rivals jockeying for position in the post-Mongka Mongol world, Hülegü decided to move a large contingent of his army from Syria back to the east, ready to fight for his share of power if necessary. He left his commander Kitbuqa behind with a much-reduced force. The moment was now opportune for a counter-offensive by the Mamluks. In early 1260, they had given an emphatic statement of intent when they summarily executed a Mongol ambassador sent to Egypt. Now, in July 1260, the Egyptian army marched north to confront the Mongols, and Sultan Qutuz sent a message to the Franks in Acre requesting safe passage and the provision of food. On the basis of the devil you know being better than the one you do not, the Franks decided to side with the Mamluks in this showdown between the two heavyweight powers of the region and agreed to Qutuz's request.

In late August the sultan learned that Kitbuqa and his Mongol army had crossed into Galilee, so he advanced his men to confront them, halting by a place called Ain Jalut. On September 3, with the bulk of his force hidden behind hills, Qutuz tempted the Mongols to charge headlong at the Mamluk vanguard under Baybars, who promptly retreated, leading the foe into the trap. Surrounded and outnumbered, the Mongols fought with their accustomed courage but were eventually downed by the Mamluks' superior numbers. The battle of Ain Jalut was a decisive and crucial victory for the Muslims; for if they had been defeated, then Egypt would almost certainly have been lost to the Mongols, and Islam, from the Nile to the Euphrates, reduced to a shadow of its former glory.

Meanwhile, back in France, Louis IX was still hankering after another crusade to the east. The years since his arrival back in France in 1254 had done nothing to dampen his affection and concern for the Latin kingdom. On his departure he had left behind a small contingent of French soldiers, whose maintenance he had paid for annually, pending his return. But, preoccupied with domestic affairs, Louis felt able to mount his second, and last, crusade only in 1267. For the next three years he raised funds and made preparations, then in 1270 he was ready to embark for the

east. In fact the destination turned out to be Tunis on the North African coastline: it seems that Louis was under the impression that the emir of Tunis was a potential Christian convert and that a convincing show of force might succeed in drawing him into the church.

Louis set sail from Aigues-Mortes in the south of France on July 2, 1270, and arrived two and a half weeks later at Carthage in Tunisia. The emir, who showed little sign of embracing Christianity, waited for the crusader attack from behind the refortified walls of Tunis. But the attack never came. While the Christians waited for reinforcements under the torrid African sun, disease – dysentery or typhus – struck their camp and thousands succumbed to illness and death. The victims included Louis himself, whose last words, fittingly, were "Jerusalem, Jerusalem!" The king's death ended the ill-fated expedition; indeed, it marked the end of large-scale, international expeditions from Europe to Outremer, which was to survive for only another 20 years.

9

ENDGAME AND AFTERMATH

At about the time that St Louis was preparing for his second crusade, to Tunis, in the late 1260s, the Franks of the Latin east were suffering from the aggressive military policy of the Mamluk leader, Sultan Rukn al-Din Baybars Bunduqdari (1260-77), the most formidable Muslim general since Saladin. The momentum generated by Baybars' ruthless campaigning and decisive victories would eventually sweep the Franks from the shores of the Holy Land for good, although Baybars himself would not live long enough to see that happen.

THE ADVANCE OF BAYBARS

Baybars came to power in 1260, shortly after the Mamluk victory over the Mongols at Ain Jalut, when, slighted by his master, Sultan Qutuz, he gained his revenge by plunging a sword in his back. His treacherous action was rewarded by his being unanimously chosen to be the next Mamluk sultan. A brilliant organizer and strategist, Baybars first of all consolidated his position of power in the Muslim world before moving against the Franks – the fact that Acre had given its support to the Mamluk cause against the Mongols carried no weight with him. Nazareth was sacked in 1263, Caesarea and Arsuf in 1265, and the Muslim frontier crept ominously closer to Acre itself. In the following year Baybars annexed Galilee but refrained from attacking Acre because of its strong garrison. Then, in 1268, the seemingly unstoppable onslaught continued when the Mamluks took Jaffa in March; two months later they captured the great city of Antioch, which had been under Christian control for 171 years. The ensuing massacre shocked even Muslim witnesses: thousands were indiscriminately butchered, while thousands more were led into captivity, dramatically deflating the price of Christian slaves. The loss of Antioch, one of the first Christian settlements in the east, had a profound effect on the Franks' morale, for it effectively meant that northern Syria no longer had a strong Christian urban centre as a focal point.

ABOVE *The bodiless heads of Christians taken prisoner by the Mamluk sultan Baybars form the focus of this 19th-century French woodcut. Baybars's reputation for ruthlessness lasted down the centuries.*

After this array of stunning victories, Baybars decided to pause for breath, and he offered the Franks a temporary truce, which they accepted with relief. Yet during this short but vital respite the Christians were unable to build up their forces or forge an effective united front against the time when hostilities would be resumed. The death in 1268 of Conradin of Hohenstaufen, the grandson of Frederick II and titular king of Jerusalem, sparked off disputes over the regency and then the kingship of the Latin kingdom. These proved to be cripplingly destabilizing, as did the ongoing rivalries and fights involving the military orders and Italian maritime republics.

But if the barons of Outremer were doing little to help their predicament, the west had not forgotten its Christian cousins in the east, even though little came of its efforts. In 1269 James I of Aragon sailed to Palestine from Spain with a large fleet. Owing to a storm, however, only a few ships reached their destination, and the small number of Spaniards who landed achieved nothing.

In the following year, King Louis made his disastrous journey to Tunis. Then in 1271, Prince Edward of England, who had been part of Louis's abortive expedition, sailed on to Palestine and landed at Acre on May 9. The prince found the situation there extremely depressing, perhaps encapsulated by the fact that the Venetians were doing a roaring trade in timber and metal for weapons – with none other than Sultan Baybars. Not only that, the Genoese were heavily involved in the Egyptian slave trade, and both Venice and Genoa had been issued licences by the high court at Acre legitimizing their actions.

Edward attempted to sort out the complexities of Outremer politics, and he tried, with little success, to form an alliance with the Mongols. He himself indulged in a few desultory raids, but his troops were far too few to be effective. The best he could do was sign a ten-year truce with Baybars, who needed to turn his attention to the threat of the Mongols, knowing that the Franks were there for the taking whenever he wanted. But in the end, Baybars decided

Left *King Edward I of England, shown here being crowned in an illustration from a work by Matthew Paris, was only a prince when he arrived in the Holy Land in 1271. A formidable warrior, Edward might have been one of the great crusaders if he had had the right resources and opportunities.*

he wanted to be rid of someone who might turn out to be a potentially formidable adversary in the future. In September 1272 he commissioned an Assassin to attack Edward, who survived and left Palestine for good. When he arrived back home he found that his father, Henry, had died and that he was no longer a prince, but the king of England.

The Waiting Game

During the 1270s, the Franks were living uneasily in an atmosphere of borrowed time. Meanwhile, in the west, attempts were still being made to rally support for the Latin kingdom. At the Second Council of Lyons in 1274, Pope Gregory X tried to conjure up a new crusade, but his subsequent elaborate and costly preparations in the end amounted to nothing. Three years later, Charles of Anjou, the brother of St Louis, who enjoyed a good diplomatic relationship with Baybars, bought the right to be the titular king of Jerusalem and sent his representative, Roger of San Severino, to govern the kingdom on his behalf. In the same year, 1277, Baybars was pursuing a largely successful campaign against the Mongols and their Muslim allies in Anatolia before eventually retiring to Syria in the face of the threat of a powerful Mongol army. There, on July 1, he died – exactly how is not known, although one persistent rumour was that he unwittingly drank from a poisoned cup intended for one of his opponents.

Jubilation among the Franks at the passing of an enemy as ruthless as Baybars lasted only as long as it took for the next Mamluk scourge of the Christians, Qalawun, to assume the reins of power in the summer of 1279. Two years later, the Franks, as fractious and divided as ever, had the opportunity of allying themselves with the Mongol leader Abaga, who had decided to invade Syria and destroy the Mamluks. But apart from the Hospitallers, the Christians decided to sign a treaty with Qalawun, and the chance to defeat their most dangerous enemy passed. As it turned out, the Mongol army, bolstered by the presence of the Hospitallers, met the Mamluk host near Homs on October 30, 1281, and in a bloody, hard-fought battle, with heavy losses on both sides, the Mongols were defeated and forced back across the Euphrates. What might have happened if they had had the full backing of the Christians remains a tantalizing speculation.

The Hospitallers were to face the full force of Qalawun's wrath four years later, when their great mountain stronghold of Marqab, whose garrison included only 25 knights, was besieged by a huge Mamluk army. For a month the besiegers pounded the castle's walls with mangonels, but to little effect; and the crucial breakthrough came only when Mamluk engineers undermined one of the towers, convincing the knights that prolonged resistance was futile. In May 1285, in return for their lives, the defenders capitulated.

THE BEGINNING OF THE END

As the Franks of Acre felt the Muslim net slowly closing around them, they were also thrown into a leadership crisis when news reached them of the death of Charles of Anjou, who was technically their king, although he had never set foot in the Latin east. The situation was resolved when Henry II, the young king of Cyprus, was offered the crown, and his coronation at Tyre on August 15, 1286, was a joyful event, followed by great festivities, with tournaments, pageants, games, feasts and dances lifting the spirits of everyone involved. But as the laughter and music faded away, the grim reality reasserted itself, and the countdown to perdition continued.

In the spring of 1287, a Mongol ambassador was making his way to western Europe to try to forge an anti-Muslim alliance – his attempts would stir the interest but not the actions of Europe's great and good. Meanwhile, the Franks had to witness the spectacle of the Genoese and Pisans fighting each other along the Syrian coast, at a time when they should have been burying their differences for the common weal. And in April Qalawun's forces, breaking a truce with the Christians, captured the port of Latakia in northern Syria, after it had been badly damaged by an earthquake. The pressure on the Franks increased even more two years later when Qalawun took the important seaport of Tripoli on April 26, 1289 – the citizens were butchered or enslaved and the city was razed to the ground. If the Christians of Acre had had any doubts about Qalawun's intentions to drive them from Palestine, surely now they must have been dispelled. Even so, a few days after Tripoli's fall, King Henry of Cyprus and Jerusalem managed to renew the truce with

Qalawun, but the king's evident lack of trust in the sultan prompted him to send an envoy to Europe to beg for help.

The leaders of the west, however, were too preoccupied with their own internal affairs to come to Outremer's rescue. The only positive response came from the common people of northern Italy. What turned out to be a rabble of peasants and townsfolk was transported to Palestine in Venetian galleys funded by the papal treasury (despite the pope's misgivings). When the Italians arrived at Acre in August 1290, they were shocked to see that Christians and Muslims were mingling freely together for commercial reasons, a state of affairs not uncommon in the Latin east during the gaps between intensive warfare. The Italians, itching to fight the infidel, which was, after all, the purpose of their taking the cross, did not take long to indulge in killing some of Acre's Muslims. The Frankish authorities were outraged by the behaviour of their co-religionists, but it was too late: Qalawun had been given his excuse for the final push.

ABOVE *Acre as it was in 1291*

THE INEVITABLE ONSLAUGHT

In November 1290, Qalawun marched from Egypt at the head of an enormous army, having taking a vow, it is said, to kill every single Christian in Acre. He did not realize this ambition, however, because just a week after setting out he fell sick and died. But his place was taken by his able and equally ruthless son al-Ashraf Khalil, who decided to postpone the expedition to the following spring. The Christians of Acre were granted one last Christmas to celebrate, and a few months to prepare for the inevitable onslaught. It started on April 5, 1291, when Sultan al-Ashraf brought up his vast host, tens of thousands strong, before the walls of Acre, along with a magnificent array of siege engines, including two giant catapults nicknamed Victorious and Furious. Inside Acre, the defenders, who included contingents from France, England, Italy, the three military orders and the Venetians and Pisans, still had command of the sea and could receive food from Cyprus. Even so, they were vastly outnumbered by the Mamluks and were staring oblivion in the face.

On April 6, the Muslim bombardment began. Stone projectiles and small vessels containing an explosive incendiary mixture crashed against the walls or dropped on the city's streets and buildings, while thousands of arrows poured down in lethal bursts. One chronicler reported that a Christian defender who was about to throw his lance at the besiegers found it peppered with arrows before he had cast it. Two Christian sorties that were launched against the Muslim camp to raise morale and relieve the pressure failed; and the arrival of King Henry from Cyprus on May 4 with a few reinforcements did not inspire great hope. During the next two weeks, the Mamluk engineers continued their deadly work of undermining key towers in Acre's defences, and on May 16 the defenders were compelled to fall back to the inner fortifications. Two days later al-Ashraf ordered his men to attack the entire southern portion of the city's walls, concentrating their efforts on the so-called Accursed Tower. The latter soon fell, enabling the Muslims to fan out and take one of the city's gates. The fighting now spread to Acre's streets and, despite their initial heroic resistance, the Franks began fleeing to the harbour to evacuate by sea. There were too few ships, however, and panic broke out. Soldiers, priests and ordinary men, women and children struggled and scrambled to find vessels to ferry them to the galleys waiting offshore. Some ferrymen milked their desperation, charging outrageous fees, while at least one craft sank under the weight of its passengers. Inevitably, a great number of Christians were left behind and were killed or sold into slavery.

With the fall of Acre, the remaining Frankish cities folded during the following weeks. Tyre was abandoned and, after initial resistance by the Templars, Sidon fell in July, as did Beirut and Haifa. The Templars relinquished their castles of Tortosa and Athlith in August, but managed to hold on to their stronghold of Ruad, which was built on a small island off the coast by Tortosa, until the persecution of their order in France in the early fourteenth century. Like the ancient Romans after their final victory over Carthage, the Mamluks devastated the Frankish lands to ensure they were never tempted to return. They cut down orchards and vineyards and destroyed irrigation works. Outremer had become a desert, and a memory.

THE CONTINUING STRUGGLE

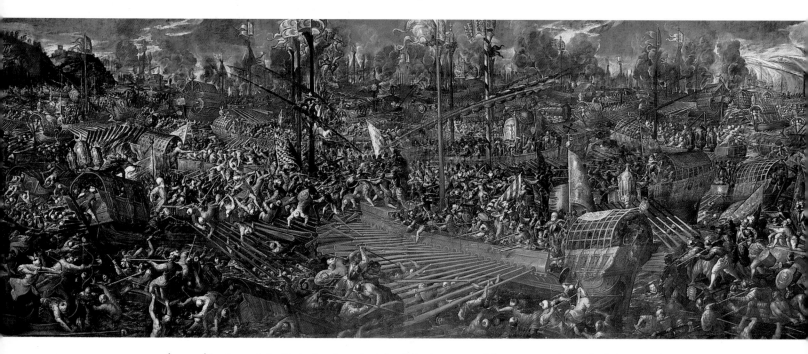

ABOVE *The naval battle of Lepanto in 1571, shown in this painting by the late 16th-century Italian artist Vicentino, was a resounding - but not decisive - victory for the Christians against the Muslims.*

The loss of the Holy Land to the Mamluks, however, did not mean the end of the crusades against the Muslims – indeed, when they did finally end is a moot point. The shattering Christian defeat against the Ottoman Turks at the battle of Nicopolis in Bulgaria in 1396 has been taken as a terminus; so too has the death of Pius II in 1464. Pius had vainly tried to galvanize Europe's princes into a crusade against the Ottomans, who had finally captured Byzantine Constantinople in 1453. He decided to lead an expedition himself, but he died before it set out and his crusade collapsed: at this point, according to Sir Steven Runciman, "The Crusading spirit was dead".

Recent research, however, has emphasized that the crusading impulse was still beating strongly in the later fifteenth and the sixteenth centuries, with frequent calls to arms by the papacy, and indulgences being given, crusade taxes raised, and the rhetoric of holy war freely employed. That little was achieved does not detract from the fact that crusades were preached and organized. To give just a few examples: in 1472, a papal-backed Christian fleet attacked and captured the Turkish towns of Smyrna and Attalia; in 1535 a Christian fleet organized by Emperor Charles V won a decisive victory against the powerful Muslim pirate Khair ad-Din Barbarossa and his forces; and in 1560 King Philip II of Spain led a crusade against Turkish-held Tripoli on the North African coastline – the expedition started brightly, but a combination of typhus and a large Turkish relief fleet resulted in a Christian disaster. Eleven years later, in 1571, Christian morale was greatly restored after the crushing naval victory of Lepanto off the coast of Greece, when a Christian armada under Don John of Austria outgunned a Turkish fleet of 275 ships.

One of the leading naval contingents among the Christian allies at Lepanto was the Knights of St John, the Hospitallers, with whom the story of the crusades draws to a close. After their expulsion from Palestine, the Hospitallers made their base on Rhodes in 1309, from where they continued offensive action against the Muslims. In 1480 the Ottoman Turks tried to drive them off the island but were fought to a standstill and eventually retired. But in 1522 Sultan Suleiman II again attacked Rhodes with a massive army and, after an epic six-month siege, finally forced the knights to surrender on honourable terms. The Hospitallers were allowed to leave their Aegean home and, for a while, they remained homeless, until Emperor Charles V gave them the sovereignty of the island of Malta in 1530. Their operations against the Turks continued, and in 1565 they heroically defended Malta against a huge Ottoman force. During the seventeenth and eighteenth centuries, however, the order gradually declined in terms of discipline as well as from a general lack of purpose. In the summer of 1798, when Napoleon Bonaparte's fleet threatened Malta while on its way to Egypt, the knights lacked the will, strength and organization to resist, and the island capitulated in two days. As historian Jonathan Riley-Smith has commented, "The crusading movement ended with the fall of Malta on June 13, 1798."

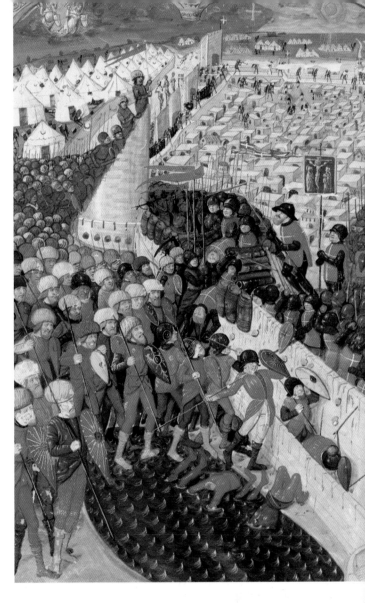

ABOVE *Rallying around a banner of Christ crucified, Knights of St John defend the walls of Rhodes against an Ottoman host in a late 15th-century French illumination.*

CONSEQUENCES OF THE CRUSADES

From a military and political perspective – that is, in terms of establishing a permanent Christian presence in Outremer – the crusades to the Latin east were ultimately a failure, even though the ability of the Franks to hang on to their settlements for 200 years was undoubtedly impressive. But they did have an important economic effect on the west. The Italian maritime republics of Venice, Genoa and Pisa were able to penetrate the commercial markets of the eastern Mediterranean and prospered at the expense of their Byzantine and Muslim counterparts; and the

wealth they created helped to stimulate the start of the Italian Renaissance.

Historians have often pointed to other less quantifiable benefits for Europe, such as the opening up of physical horizons in the east leading to a greater awareness of foreign ideas and culture, from military architecture to diet and dress. Yet it should be reiterated that the direct transmission of Muslim learning to the west came mainly through Spain and Sicily, not Outremer. Also, Europe by the start of the crusades was already beginning to enjoy an

increase in population, an expansion of trade and a new confidence – so it could be argued that the crusades were as much a symptom as a cause of this florescence. The single most significant consequence of the crusades, however, was arguably a negative one: the Franks' sack of Constantinople, for so long the great Christian bulwark against Muslim expansion in the east. Although the city was not taken by the Ottoman Turks until 1453, its capture by the crusaders critically weakened the Byzantine Empire, precipitating its decline and fall.

CHRONOLOGY

The following list of dates gives the key events of the crusades to the east. Entries in bold type indicate major episodes treated in this book.

1071   Battle of Manzikert: the Seljuk Turks destroy the Byzantine army.

1095   Pope Urban II proclaims First Crusade at the Council of Clermont.

1096   **First Crusade** begins.

1098   City of Edessa taken by Baldwin of Boulogne; Antioch falls to the crusaders.

1099   Crusaders capture Jerusalem and elect Godfrey of Bouillon as ruler of the Latin kingdom of Jerusalem.

1100   Godfrey dies and is succeeded by Baldwin I as king of Jerusalem.

1119   Battle of the Field of Blood: the Muslims inflict a heavy defeat on the Franks.

1124   Crusaders take city of Tyre.

1144   A Muslim force under Zangi captures Edessa.

1147   **Second Crusade** begins under Louis VII of France and Emperor Conrad III.

1148   Crusaders withdraw from the siege of Damascus.

1154   Nur al-Din captures Damascus.

1169   Saladin becomes vizier of Egypt, ruling it on behalf of Nur al-Din.

1174   After the death of Nur al-Din, Saladin becomes ruler of both Damascus and Egypt.

1187   Battle of Hattin: Saladin defeats King Guy and the Christians before going on to take Jerusalem.

1189   **Third Crusade** begins.

1190   Emperor Frederick I Barbarossa drowns in Cilicia.

1191   Richard I of England and Philip II of France take Acre; the crusaders under Richard defeat Saladin at the battle of Arsuf.

1192   Richard departs from the Holy Land.

1193   Saladin dies in Damascus.

1202   **Fourth Crusade** begins.

1204   Crusaders sack Constantinople and elect Baldwin of Flanders as the first Latin emperor of Constantinople.

1209   Crusade against the Albigenses of southern France begins.

1212   Battle of Las Navas de Tolosa re-ignites the *Reconquista* in Spain; Children's Crusade.

1215   Fourth Lateran Council: Pope Innocent III appeals for a crusade to the Holy Land.

1217   **Fifth Crusade** begins under Duke Leopold VI of Austria and King Andrew II of Hungary.

1219   Crusaders capture Damietta in Egypt.

1221   Crusaders defeated in Egypt and the Fifth Crusade ends in failure.

1228   **Crusade of Frederick II**.

1229   Frederick negotiates the return of Jerusalem into Christian hands.

1244   Jerusalem falls to Khwarazmian Turks.

1248   **First crusade of King Louis IX of France** begins.

1249   King Louis captures Damietta.

1250   Crusaders defeated in Egypt and Louis is taken captive.

1251   Shepherds' Crusade in France.

1254   King Louis returns to France from Outremer.

1258   A Mongol army under Hülegü sacks Baghdad.

1260   The Mongols are defeated at Ain Jalut by the Mamluks; Baybars becomes sultan of Egypt.

1268   Antioch falls to the Mamluks.

1270   **Second Crusade of Louis IX**; he dies of an illness in Tunisia.

1277   Death of Baybars, Mamluk sultan of Egypt.

1289   The Mamluks take Tripoli.

1291   The fall of Acre to the Mamluks signals end of Christian settlements in Outremer.

BIOGRAPHIES

This list is intended as a brief aide-mémoire of some of the more important figures to feature in the crusades to the east.

Alexius I Comnenus
Byzantine emperor (1081–1118) whose appeal to Pope Urban II helped to start the First Crusade. His largely successful attempt to get the crusaders to swear an oath of fealty to him in the end bore little fruit. But his 37-year reign strengthened the empire, which had been weak and vulnerable at his accession.

Alexius IV Angelus
The son of Byzantine emperor Isaac II Angelus, Alexius was a key figure in the Fourth Crusade. He persuaded the crusaders to restore him to the throne of Constantinople in return for a substantial amount of money and other rewards. His inability to fulfil his side of the bargain prompted the crusaders' sack of Constantinople in 1204.

Baldwin I
Brother of Godfrey of Bouillon, Baldwin became king of Jerusalem in 1100, having already founded the county of Edessa. He stabilized the nascent Latin kingdom until his death in 1118.

Baldwin II
The second king of Jerusalem was the cousin of his namesake, Baldwin I, and his reign (1118–31) coincided with a resurgence of Muslim military endeavour in Syria. After his death, his daughter, Melisende, and her husband, Fulk of Anjou, ruled the Latin kingdom.

Baybars
The Mamluk sultan first came to prominence during Louis IX's crusade in Egypt. After the assassination of Sultan Qutuz in 1260, Baybars assumed the leadership of the Mamluks and proved to be a formidable soldier, capturing a number of towns and castles from the Franks, including Antioch in 1268.

Bernard of Clairvaux
One of the great churchmen of his time, Bernard was a Cistercian monk who preached the Second Crusade with great effect in 1145. The failure of the expedition, however, severely damaged his reputation.

Bohemond of Taranto
A tough, astute Norman warrior, Bohemond became prince of Antioch in 1098, having masterminded its capture from the Muslims. In 1100 he was imprisoned by the Muslim emir of Aleppo for three years; and in 1108, back in the west, he attacked but failed to capture a Byzantine port, after which he was forced to pay homage to Emperor Alexius I.

Conrad III
Founder of the Hohenstaufen dynasty, Conrad became king of Germany in 1138 and was one of the leaders of the Second Crusade. After a heavy defeat by the Turks in Anatolia, Conrad eventually managed to reach Palestine, where he joined forces with Louis VII. But their attack on Damascus ended in failure.

Conrad of Montferrat

After the disastrous Christian defeat at the battle of Hattin in 1187, it was Conrad who organized the defence of Tyre with great effect. He was eventually asked to become king of Jerusalem, but his reign was cut short by his death at the hands of an Assassin.

Dandolo, Enrico

The doge of Venice since 1193, Dandolo was well advanced in years when the opportunity arose for him to play a leading role in the Fourth Crusade. His canniness, diplomatic skills and physical bravery were instrumental in the crusaders' capture and sack of Constantinople in 1204, from which Venice drew great profit.

Frederick I Barbarossa

The Holy Roman Emperor was probably the most respected ruler in Europe when he embarked on the Third Crusade with a huge German army. His efforts came to nothing when he drowned in a river in Cilicia.

Frederick II

The grandson of Frederick Barbarossa, Frederick took the cross in 1215 but only sailed to Outremer in 1228. By skilful diplomacy he managed to regain Jerusalem from the Muslims, but the strategic position of the city remained extremely precarious.

Godfrey of Bouillon

The duke of Lower Lorraine was one of the leaders of the First Crusade. After the capture of Jerusalem in 1099 he was offered the crown but preferred to rule as "Advocate of the Holy Sepulchre". He died in 1100 and was succeeded by his brother Baldwin of Boulogne, the count of Edessa.

Guy of Lusignan

Originally from Poitou in France, Guy gained access to the throne of Jerusalem by way of his marriage to Sybilla, the sister of King Baldwin IV. After his defeat and capture at the battle of Hattin and subsequent release, Guy vied with Conrad of Montferrat for the kingship of the Latin kingdom. In the end he had to settle for the throne of Cyprus in 1192.

Ilghazi

As prince of Aleppo, Ilghazi – a Seljuk Turk by birth – routed the Franks at the battle of the Field of Blood in 1119. In doing so he set in motion the first ripples of a concerted Muslim counter-offensive against the Christian settlers.

Innocent III

One of the great popes of the Middle Ages, Innocent was a crusades enthusiast. He was initially furious that the Fourth Crusade was diverted from Egypt to Constantinople, but then hoped it might lead to the Catholic Church being reunited with the Greek Orthodox Church. He also inaugurated the Albigensian Crusade, and his efforts to launch another great expedition to the east resulted in the Fifth Crusade, although he did not live to witness it.

Isaac II Angelus

This weak and elderly Byzantine emperor was deposed by his brother, Alexius III, in 1195 and blinded and thrown into prison. After the flight of Alexius during the Fourth Crusade, Isaac ruled again for a short while with his son, Alexius IV, before again being deposed and probably murdered.

John of Brienne

A French nobleman, John became king of Jerusalem in 1210 through his marriage to Maria, the hereditary queen of the kingdom. He later unsuccessfully disputed the right to be regent of the kingdom with Frederick II after the latter married his daughter Isabella. John eventually became Latin emperor of Constantinople in 1231.

Al-Kamil

The Ayubid sultan of Egypt, al-Kamil was instrumental in repulsing the crusaders' invasion of his country during the Fifth Crusade. He was also a key figure in Frederick II's crusade, when he negotiated the return of Jerusalem (and other places) to the Christians in return for the emperor's evacuation of Outremer.

Louis VII

The king of France was one of the leaders of the Second Crusade, which failed to capture the city of Damascus. He and his wife Eleanor of Aquitaine divorced in 1152 and she went on to marry his great rival, Henry II of England.

Louis IX

Renowned for his justice and piety, the French king Louis launched a crusade against the Muslims of Egypt but was eventually defeated and captured in 1249. Freed after the payment of a huge ransom, he organized the affairs of Outremer before returning to France. He launched a second crusade against Tunis in 1270, but died while on campaign.

Nur al-Din

One of the most effective and powerful of Muslim leaders in the Near East, Nur al-Din was the son of Zangi, the emir of Mosul and Aleppo. He united the Muslims of Syria and during the 1160s became involved in the politics of Egypt, which he eventually ruled, at least nominally, through his lieutenant Saladin.

Peter the Hermit

One of the leaders of the People's Crusade, Peter survived its destruction and then travelled with the main army of the First Crusade. He unsuccessfully tried to desert during the siege of Antioch, but he did go on to witness the capture of Jerusalem. After returning to Europe he became prior of a monastery in the Low Countries.

Philip II Augustus

One of the leaders of the Third Crusade, the French king Philip was more of an astute politician than a heroic general. He left the crusade after the fall of Acre in 1191 and, back home, intrigued against his rival and co-leader of the crusade, Richard I of England.

Raymond of St Gilles, Count of Toulouse

One of the most respected generals of the First Crusade, Raymond was offered the crown of Jerusalem, but declined to take it. He went on to establish the county of Tripoli.

Richard I

Arguably the best general of the crusading era, Richard succeeded his father, Henry II, as king of England in 1189 and was the leading figure of the Third Crusade. Despite local victories, however, he failed to recapture Jerusalem from Saladin.

Saladin

Renowned for his justice, honesty and chivalry, Saladin was perhaps the greatest Muslim figure of the crusades. A Kurd by birth, he gained control of Egypt and Syria, and recaptured Jerusalem from the Christians after the battle of Hattin in 1187. After his death in 1193 his empire was divided up between his sons.

Tancred

A Norman by birth, Tancred was the nephew of Bohemond, one of the leaders of the First Crusade. After the conquest of Jerusalem he was appointed prince of Galilee and he later ruled Antioch during the imprisonment of Bohemond by the Muslims.

Urban II

A notable reforming pope, Urban responded to pleas for help from the Byzantine emperor Alexius I and vigorously preached the First Crusade. He died before hearing of the capture of Jerusalem in the summer of 1099.

Zangi

Emir of Mosul and Aleppo, Zangi was a formidable opponent of the Franks and eventually captured Edessa in 1144, thus prompting the Second Crusade. His victories over the Christian settlers brought him renown in the Muslim world, but in 1146 he was murdered by a member of his court.

BIBLIOGRAPHY

The following list represents a selection of the works used in the writing of this book as well as suggestions for further reading. Short, accessible accounts of the crusades to the east have been written by Antony Bridge and Malcolm Billings. Sir Steven Runciman's three-volume history is still an indispensable work, detailed, scholarly and entertaining. For more up-to-date scholarship and analysis, the works of Jonathan Riley-Smith are recommended. For a Muslim perspective of the crusades Amin Maalouf is a good guide.

Billings, Malcolm *The Cross and the Crescent: A History of the Crusades* London: BBC Publications, 1987

Boase, T.S.R. *Castles and Churches of the Crusader Kingdom* Oxford: Oxford University Press, 1967

Bridge, Antony *The Crusades* London: Granada, 1980

Cohn, Norman *The Pursuit of the Millennium* London: Pimlico, 1993

Comnena, Anna *The Alexiad* tr. E.R.A. Sewter, London: Penguin Books, 1969

Fletcher, Richard *The Cross and the Crescent* London: Penguin Books, 2003

Hallam, Elizabeth (ed.) *Chronicles of the Crusades: Eye-witness Accounts of the Wars between Christianity and Islam*
        London: Weidenfeld and Nicolson, 1989

Harpur, James *Sacred Tracks: 2000 Years of Christian Pilgrimage* London: Frances Lincoln, 2001

Hillenbrand, Carole *The Crusades: Islamic Perspectives* Edinburgh: Edinburgh University Press, 1999

Joinville, John of, and Villehardouin, Geoffrey of, *Chronicles of the Crusades* tr. M.R.B. Shaw, London:
        Penguin Books, 1969

Jones, Terry and Ereira, Alan *The Crusades* London: Penguin Books, 1996

Kennedy, Hugh *Crusader Castles* Cambridge: Cambridge University Press, 1994

Maalouf, Amin *The Crusades through Arab Eyes* tr. Jon Rothschild, London: Al Saqi Books, 1984

Marshall, Christopher *Warfare in the Latin East, 1192–1291* Cambridge: Cambridge University Press, 1992

Mayer, Hans Eberhard *The Crusades* tr. J Gillingham (2nd edn), Oxford: Oxford University Press, 1988

McManners, John (ed.) *The Oxford History of Christianity*, Oxford: Oxford University Press, 1993

Norwich, John Julius *Byzantium: The Decline and Fall* London: Penguin Books, 1996

Prawer, Joshua *The Latin Kingdom of Jerusalem* London: Weidenfeld and Nicolson, 1972

Riley-Smith, J.S.C. *The First Crusade and the Idea of Crusading* London: Athlone Press, 1986

        —*The Crusades: A Short History* London: Athlone Press, 1990

        —*The Atlas of the Crusades* London: Times Books, 1991

        — (ed.) *The Oxford Illustrated History of the Crusades* Oxford: Oxford University Press, 1995

Riley-Smith, J.S.C and L. *The Crusades: Idea and Reality 1095–1274* London: Edward Arnold, 1981

Runciman, Steven *A History of the Crusades*, 3 vols., Harmondsworth: Penguin Books, 1965

Smail, R.C. *Crusading Warfare 1097–1193* Cambridge: Cambridge University Press, 1956

Southern, R.W. *The Making of the Middle Ages* London: Arrow Books, 1959

Sumption, Jonathan *The Albigensian Crusade* London: Faber & Faber, 1978

Trevor-Roper, Hugh *The Rise of Christian Europe* London: Thames and Hudson, 1966

Vryonis, Speros *Byzantium and Europe* London: Thames and Hudson, 1967

INDEX

PICTURE CREDITS